DATE DUE

DEMCO 38-296

ANTIPHON & ANDOCIDES

THE ORATORY OF CLASSICAL GREECE

Translated with Notes • *Michael Gagarin, Series Editor*

VOLUME I

ANTIPHON & ANDOCIDES

Translated by Michael Gagarin & Douglas M. MacDowell

 UNIVERSITY OF TEXAS PRESS, AUSTIN

The publication of this book was assisted by a
University Cooperative Society Subvention Grant
awarded by the University of Texas at Austin.

First edition, 1998

⊗ The paper used in this publication meets
the minimum requirements of American National
Standard for Information Sciences—Permanence of
Paper for Printed Library Materials, ANSI Z39.48-1984.

Library of Congress Cataloging-in-Publication Data

Antiphon, ca. 480–411 B.C.
    Antiphon and Andocides / translated by Michael
Gagarin and Douglas M. MacDowell. — 1st ed.
        p.   cm. — (The oratory of classical
Greece ; v. 1)
    English translations of classical Greek orations of
Antiphon and Andocides.
    Includes bibliographical references and index.
    ISBN 0-292-72808-5 (alk. paper). —
    ISBN 0-292-72809-3 (pbk. : alk. paper)
    1. Antiphon, ca. 480–411 B.C.—Translations into
English.   2. Andocides, ca. 440–390 B.C.—Translations
into English.   3. Speeches, addresses, etc., Greek—
Translations into English.   4. Oratory, Ancient.
I. Andocides, ca. 440–ca. 390 B.C.   II. Gagarin,
Michael.   III. MacDowell, Douglas M. (Douglas
Maurice)   IV. Title.   V. Series.
PA3869.A3   1998
885'.01—dc21   97-21207

CONTENTS

〜〜〜

PREFACE

This is the first volume in a series of translations of *The Oratory of Classical Greece*. The aim of the series is to make available primarily for those who do not read Greek up-to-date, accurate, and readable translations with introductions and explanatory notes of all the surviving works and major fragments of the Attic orators of the classical period (ca. 420–320 BC): Aeschines, Andocides, Antiphon, Demosthenes, Dinarchus, Hyperides, Isaeus, Isocrates, Lycurgus, and Lysias.

I am grateful for the support this series has received from my fellow translators, from colleagues in the field, and from everyone at the University of Texas Press. Director Joanna Hitchcock encouraged the project from the beginning, when it was only a vague idea; Humanities Editor Ali Hossaini and his successor, Jim Burr, have been very supportive and helpful with numerous aspects of the project; and the staff, including Carolyn Wylie and copyeditor Nancy Moore, have been constructively helpful.

Publication of this first volume has been assisted by a subvention grant from the University Cooperative Society, awarded by the University of Texas at Austin. The Coop is to be commended for its cooperation with and support of the University of Texas faculty.

—M. G.

SERIES INTRODUCTION
Greek Oratory

‹‹‹

By Michael Gagarin

ORATORY IN CLASSICAL ATHENS

From as early as Homer (and undoubtedly much earlier) the Greeks placed a high value on effective speaking. Even Achilles, whose greatness was primarily established on the battlefield, was brought up to be "a speaker of words and a doer of deeds" (*Iliad* 9.443); and Athenian leaders of the sixth and fifth centuries,[1] such as Solon, Themistocles, and Pericles, were all accomplished orators. Most Greek literary genres—notably epic, tragedy, and history—underscore the importance of oratory by their inclusion of set speeches. The formal pleadings of the envoys to Achilles in the *Iliad*, the messenger speeches in tragedy reporting events like the battle of Salamis in Aeschylus' *Persians* or the gruesome death of Pentheus in Euripides' *Bacchae*, and the powerful political oratory of Pericles' funeral oration in Thucydides are but a few of the most notable examples of the Greeks' never-ending fascination with formal public speaking, which was to reach its height in the public oratory of the fourth century.

In early times, oratory was not a specialized subject of study but was learned by practice and example. The formal study of rhetoric as an "art" (*technē*) began, we are told, in the middle of the fifth century in Sicily with the work of Corax and his pupil Tisias.[2] These two are

---

[1] All dates in this volume are BC unless the contrary is either indicated or obvious.

[2] See Kennedy 1963: 26–51. Cole 1991 has challenged this traditional picture, arguing that the term "rhetoric" was coined by Plato to designate and denigrate an activity he strongly opposed. Cole's own reconstruction is not without prob-

scarcely more than names to us, but another famous Sicilian, Gorgias of Leontini (ca. 490–390), developed a new style of argument and is reported to have dazzled the Athenians with a speech delivered when he visited Athens in 427. Gorgias initiated the practice, which continued into the early fourth century, of composing speeches for mythical or imaginary occasions. The surviving examples reveal a lively intellectual climate in the late fifth and early fourth centuries, in which oratory served to display new ideas, new forms of expression, and new methods of argument.[3] This tradition of "intellectual" oratory was continued by the fourth-century educator Isocrates and played a large role in later Greek and Roman education.

In addition to this intellectual oratory, at about the same time the practice also began of writing speeches for real occasions in public life, which we may designate "practical" oratory. For centuries Athenians had been delivering speeches in public settings (primarily the courts and the Assembly), but these had always been composed and delivered impromptu, without being written down and thus without being preserved. The practice of writing speeches began in the courts and then expanded to include the Assembly and other settings. Athens was one of the leading cities of Greece in the fifth and fourth centuries, and its political and legal systems depended on direct participation by a large number of citizens; all important decisions were made by these large bodies, and the primary means of influencing these decisions was oratory.[4] Thus, it is not surprising that oratory flourished in Athens,[5] but it may not be immediately obvious why it should be written down.

The pivotal figure in this development was Antiphon, one of the fifth-century intellectuals who are often grouped together under the

---

lems, but he does well to remind us how thoroughly the traditional view of rhetoric depends on one of its most ardent opponents.

[3] Of these only Antiphon's Tetralogies are included in this series. Gorgias' *Helen* and *Palamedes*, Alcidamas' *Odysseus*, and Antisthenes' *Ajax* and *Odysseus* are translated in Gagarin and Woodruff 1995.

[4] Yunis 1996 has a good treatment of political oratory from Pericles to Demosthenes.

[5] All our evidence for practical oratory comes from Athens, with the exception of Isocrates 19, written for a trial in Aegina. Many speeches were undoubtedly delivered in courts and political forums in other Greek cities, but it may be that such speeches were written down only in Athens.

name "Sophists." [6] Like some of the other sophists he contributed to the intellectual oratory of the period, but he also had a strong practical interest in law. At the same time, Antiphon had an aversion to public speaking and did not directly involve himself in legal or political affairs (Thucydides 8.68). However, he began giving general advice to other citizens who were engaged in litigation and were thus expected to address the court themselves. As this practice grew, Antiphon went further, and around 430 he began writing out whole speeches for others to memorize and deliver. Thus began the practice of "logography," which continued through the next century and beyond.[7] Logography particularly appealed to men like Lysias, who were metics, or noncitizen residents of Athens. Since they were not Athenian citizens, they were barred from direct participation in public life, but they could contribute by writing speeches for others.

Antiphon was also the first (to our knowledge) to write down a speech he would himself deliver, writing the speech for his own defense at his trial for treason in 411. His motive was probably to publicize and preserve his views, and others continued this practice of writing down speeches they would themselves deliver in the courts and (more rarely) the Assembly.[8] Finally, one other type of practical oratory was the special tribute delivered on certain important public occasions, the best known of which is the funeral oration. It is convenient to designate these three types of oratory by the terms Aristotle later uses: forensic (for the courts), deliberative (for the Assembly), and epideictic (for display).[9]

---

[6] The term "sophist" was loosely used through the fifth and fourth centuries to designate various intellectuals and orators, but under the influence of Plato, who attacked certain figures under this name, the term is now used of a specific group of thinkers; see Kerferd 1981.

[7] For Antiphon as the first to write speeches, see Photius, *Bibliotheca* 486a7–11 and [Plut.], *Moralia* 832c–d. The latest extant speech can be dated to 320, but we know that at least one orator, Dinarchus, continued the practice after that date.

[8] Unlike forensic speeches, speeches for delivery in the Assembly were usually not composed beforehand in writing, since the speaker could not know exactly when or in what context he would be speaking; see further Trevett 1996.

[9] *Rhetoric* 1.3. Intellectual orations, like Gorgias' *Helen*, do not easily fit into Aristotle's classification. For a fuller (but still brief) introduction to Attic oratory and the orators, see Edwards 1994.

THE ORATORS

In the century from about 420 to 320, dozens—perhaps even hundreds—of now unknown orators and logographers must have composed speeches that are now lost, but only ten of these men were selected for preservation and study by ancient scholars, and only works collected under the names of these ten have been preserved. Some of these works are undoubtedly spurious, though in most cases they are fourth-century works by a different author rather than later "forgeries." Indeed, modern scholars suspect that as many as seven of the speeches attributed to Demosthenes may have been written by Apollodorus, son of Pasion, who is sometimes called "the eleventh orator." [10] Including these speeches among the works of Demosthenes may have been an honest mistake, or perhaps a bookseller felt he could sell more copies of these speeches if they were attributed to a more famous orator.

In alphabetical order the Ten Orators are as follows: [11]

- AESCHINES (ca. 395–ca. 322) rose from obscure origins to become an important Athenian political figure, first an ally, then a bitter enemy of Demosthenes. His three speeches all concern major public issues. The best known of these (Aes. 3) was delivered at the trial in 330, when Demosthenes responded with *On the Crown* (Dem. 18). Aeschines lost the case and was forced to leave Athens and live the rest of his life in exile.

- ANDOCIDES (ca. 440–ca. 390) is best known for his role in the scandal of 415, when just before the departure of the fateful Athenian expedition to Sicily during the Peloponnesian War (431–404), a band of young men mutilated statues of Hermes, and at the same time information was revealed about the secret rites of Demeter.

---

[10] See Trevett 1992.

[11] The Loeb volumes of *Minor Attic Orators* also include the prominent Athenian political figure Demades (ca. 385–319), who was not one of the Ten; but the only speech that has come down to us under his name is a later forgery. It is possible that Demades and other fourth-century politicians who had a high reputation for public speaking did not put any speeches in writing, especially if they rarely spoke in the courts (see above n. 8).

Andocides was exiled but later returned. Two of the four speeches in his name give us a contemporary view of the scandal: one pleads for his return, the other argues against a second period of exile.

• ANTIPHON (ca. 480–411), as already noted, wrote forensic speeches for others and only once spoke himself. In 411 he participated in an oligarchic coup by a group of 400, and when the democrats regained power he was tried for treason and executed. His six surviving speeches include three for delivery in court and the three Tetralogies—imaginary intellectual exercises for display or teaching that consist of four speeches each, two on each side. All six of Antiphon's speeches concern homicide, probably because these stood at the beginning of the collection of his works. Fragments of some thirty other speeches cover many different topics.

• DEMOSTHENES (384–322) is generally considered the best of the Attic orators. Although his nationalistic message is less highly regarded today, his powerful mastery of and ability to combine many different rhetorical styles continues to impress readers. Demosthenes was still a child when his wealthy father died. The trustees of the estate apparently misappropriated much of it, and when he came of age, he sued them in a series of cases (27–31), regaining some of his fortune and making a name as a powerful speaker. He then wrote speeches for others in a variety of cases, public and private, and for his own use in court (where many cases involved major public issues), and in the Assembly, where he opposed the growing power of Philip of Macedon. The triumph of Philip and his son Alexander the Great eventually put an end to Demosthenes' career. Some sixty speeches have come down under his name, about a third of them of questionable authenticity.

• DINARCHUS (ca. 360–ca. 290) was born in Corinth but spent much of his life in Athens as a metic (a noncitizen resident). His public fame came primarily from writing speeches for the prosecutions surrounding the Harpalus affair in 324, when several prominent figures (including Demosthenes) were accused of bribery. After 322 he had a profitable career as a logographer.

• HYPERIDES (390–322) was a political leader and logographer of so many different talents that he was called the pentathlete of orators.

He was a leader of the Athenian resistance to Philip and Alexander and (like Demosthenes) was condemned to death after Athens' final surrender. One speech and substantial fragments of five others have been recovered from papyrus remains; otherwise, only fragments survive.

• ISAEUS (ca. 415–ca. 340) wrote speeches on a wide range of topics, but the eleven complete speeches that survive, dating from ca. 390 to ca. 344, all concern inheritance. As with Antiphon, the survival of these particular speeches may have been the result of the later ordering of his speeches by subject; we have part of a twelfth speech and fragments and titles of some forty other works. Isaeus is said to have been a pupil of Isocrates and the teacher of Demosthenes.

• ISOCRATES (436–338) considered himself a philosopher and educator, not an orator or rhetorician. He came from a wealthy Athenian family but lost most of his property in the Peloponnesian War, and in 403 he took up logography. About 390 he abandoned this practice and turned to writing and teaching, setting forth his educational, philosophical, and political views in essays that took the form of speeches but were not meant for oral delivery. He favored accommodation with the growing power of Philip of Macedon and panhellenic unity. His school was based on a broad concept of rhetoric and applied philosophy; it attracted pupils from the entire Greek world (including Isaeus, Lycurgus, and Hyperides) and became the main rival of Plato's Academy. Isocrates greatly influenced education and rhetoric in the Hellenistic, Roman, and modern periods until the eighteenth century.

• LYCURGUS (ca. 390–ca. 324) was a leading public official who restored the financial condition of Athens after 338 and played a large role in the city for the next dozen years. He brought charges of corruption or treason against many other officials, usually with success. Only one speech survives.

• LYSIAS (ca. 445–ca. 380) was a metic—an official resident of Athens but not a citizen. Much of his property was seized by the Thirty during their short-lived oligarchic coup in 404–403. Perhaps as a result he turned to logography. More than thirty speeches survive in whole or in part, though the authenticity of some is doubted.

We also have fragments or know the titles of more than a hundred others. The speeches cover a wide range of cases, and he may have delivered one himself (Lys. 12), on the death of his brother at the hands of the Thirty. Lysias is particularly known for his vivid narratives, his *ēthopoiïa*, or "creation of character," and his prose style, which became a model of clarity and vividness.

THE WORKS OF THE ORATORS

As soon as speeches began to be written down, they could be preserved. We know little about the conditions of book "publication" (i.e., making copies for distribution) in the fourth century, but there was an active market for books in Athens, and some of the speeches may have achieved wide circulation.[12] An orator (or his family) may have preserved his own speeches, perhaps to advertise his ability or demonstrate his success, or booksellers may have collected and copied them in order to make money.

We do not know how closely the preserved text of these speeches corresponded to the version actually delivered in court or in the Assembly. Speakers undoubtedly extemporized or varied from their text on occasion, but there is no good evidence that deliberative speeches were substantially revised for publication.[13] In forensic oratory a logographer's reputation would derive first and foremost from his success with jurors. If a forensic speech was victorious, there would be no reason to alter it for publication, and if it lost, alteration would probably not deceive potential clients. Thus, the published texts of forensic speeches were probably quite faithful to the texts that were provided to clients, and we have little reason to suspect substantial alteration in the century or so before they were collected by scholars in Alexandria (see below).

In addition to the speaker's text, most forensic speeches have breaks for the inclusion of documents. The logographer inserted a notation

---

[12] Dover's discussion (1968) of the preservation and transmission of the works of Lysias (and perhaps others under his name) is useful not just for Lysias but for the other orators too. His theory of shared authorship between logographer and litigant, however, is unconvincing (see Usher 1976).

[13] See further Trevett 1996: 437–439.

in his text—such as *nomos* ("law") or *martyria* ("testimony")—and the speaker would pause while the clerk read out the text of a law or the testimony of witnesses. Many speeches survive with only a notation that a *nomos* or *martyria* was read at that point, but in some cases the text of the document is included. It used to be thought that these documents were all creations of later scholars, but many (though not all) are now accepted as genuine.[14]

With the foundation of the famous library in Alexandria early in the third century, scholars began to collect and catalogue texts of the orators, along with many other classical authors. Only the best orators were preserved in the library, many of them represented by over 100 speeches each (some undoubtedly spurious). Only some of these works survived in manuscript form to the modern era; more recently a few others have been discovered on ancient sheets of papyrus, so that today the corpus of Attic Oratory consists of about 150 speeches, together with a few letters and other works. The subject matter ranges from important public issues and serious crimes to business affairs, lovers' quarrels, inheritance disputes, and other personal or family matters.

In the centuries after these works were collected, ancient scholars gathered biographical facts about their authors, produced grammatical and lexicographic notes, and used some of the speeches as evidence for Athenian political history. But the ancient scholars who were most interested in the orators were those who studied prose style, the most notable of these being Dionysius of Halicarnassus (first century BC), who wrote treatises on several of the orators,[15] and Hermogenes of Tarsus (second century AD), who wrote several literary studies, including *On Types of Style*.[16] But relative to epic or tragedy, oratory was little studied; and even scholars of rhetoric whose interests were broader than style, like Cicero and Quintilian, paid little attention to the orators, except for the acknowledged master, Demosthenes.

Most modern scholars until the second half of the twentieth century continued to treat the orators primarily as prose stylists.[17] The

---

[14] See MacDowell 1990: 43–47; Todd 1993: 44–45.

[15] Dionysius' literary studies are collected and translated in Usher 1974–1985.

[16] Wooten 1987. Stylistic considerations probably also influenced the selection of the "canon" of ten orators; see Worthington 1994.

[17] For example, the most popular and influential book ever written on the orators, Jebb's *The Attic Orators* (1875) was presented as an "attempt to aid in giving

reevaluation of Athenian democracy by George Grote and others in the nineteenth century stimulated renewed interest in Greek oratory among historians; and increasing interest in Athenian law during that century led a few legal scholars to read the orators. But in comparison with the interest shown in the other literary genres—epic, lyric, tragedy, comedy, and even history—Attic oratory has been relatively neglected until the last third of the twentieth century. More recently, however, scholars have discovered the value of the orators for the broader study of Athenian culture and society. Since Dover's groundbreaking works on popular morality and homosexuality,[18] interest in the orators has been increasing rapidly, and they are now seen as primary representatives of Athenian moral and social values, and as evidence for social and economic conditions, political and social ideology, and in general those aspects of Athenian culture that in the past were commonly ignored by historians of ancient Greece but are of increasing interest and importance today, including women and the family, slavery, and the economy.

GOVERNMENT AND LAW IN CLASSICAL ATHENS

The hallmark of the Athenian political and legal systems was its amateurism. Most public officials, including those who supervised the courts, were selected by lot and held office for a limited period, typically a year. Thus a great many citizens held public office at some point in their lives, but almost none served for an extended period of time or developed the experience or expertise that would make them professionals. All significant policy decisions were debated and voted on in the Assembly, where the quorum was 6,000 citizens, and all significant legal cases were judged by bodies of 200 to 500 jurors or more. Public prominence was not achieved by election (or selection) to public office but depended rather on a man's ability to sway the

---

Attic Oratory its due place in the history of Attic Prose" (I.xiii). This modern focus on prose style can plausibly be connected to the large role played by prose composition (the translation of English prose into Greek, usually in imitation of specific authors or styles) in the Classics curriculum, especially in Britain.

[18] Dover (1974, 1978). Dover recently commented (1994: 157), "When I began to mine the riches of Attic forensic oratory I was astonished to discover that the mine had never been exploited."

majority of citizens in the Assembly or jurors in court to vote in favor of a proposed course of action or for one of the litigants in a trial. Success was never permanent, and a victory on one policy issue or a verdict in one case could be quickly reversed in another.[19] In such a system the value of public oratory is obvious, and in the fourth century, oratory became the most important cultural institution in Athens, replacing drama as the forum where major ideological concerns were displayed and debated.

Several recent books give good detailed accounts of Athenian government and law,[20] and so a brief sketch can suffice here. The main policy-making body was the Assembly, open to all adult male citizens; a small payment for attendance enabled at least some of the poor to attend along with the leisured rich. In addition, a Council of 500 citizens, selected each year by lot with no one allowed to serve more than two years, prepared material for and made recommendations to the Assembly; a rotating subgroup of this Council served as an executive committee, the Prytany. Finally, numerous officials, most of them selected by lot for one-year terms, supervised different areas of administration and finance. The most important of these were the nine Archons (lit. "rulers"): the eponymous Archon after whom the year was named, the Basileus ("king"),[21] the Polemarch, and the six Thesmothetae. Councilors and almost all these officials underwent a preliminary examination (*dokimasia*) before taking office, and officials submitted to a final accounting (*euthynai*) upon leaving; at these times any citi-

---

[19] In the Assembly this could be accomplished by a reconsideration of the question, as in the famous Mytilenean debate (Thuc. 3.36–50); in court a verdict was final, but its practical effects could be thwarted or reversed by later litigation on a related issue.

[20] For government, see Sinclair 1988, Hansen 1991; for law, MacDowell 1978, Todd 1993, and Boegehold 1995 (Bonner 1927 is still helpful). Much of our information about the legal and political systems comes from a work attributed to Aristotle but perhaps written by a pupil of his, *The Athenian Constitution* (*Ath. Pol.*—conveniently translated with notes by Rhodes 1984). The discovery of this work on a papyrus in Egypt in 1890 caused a major resurgence of interest in Athenian government.

[21] Modern scholars often use the term *archōn basileus* or "king archon," but Athenian sources (e.g., *Ath. Pol.* 57) simply call him the *basileus*.

zen who wished could challenge a person's fitness for his new position or his performance in his recent position.

There was no general taxation of Athenian citizens. Sources of public funding included the annual tax levied on metics, various fees and import duties, and (in the fifth century) tribute from allied cities; but the source that figures most prominently in the orators is the Athenian system of liturgies (*leitourgiai*), by which in a regular rotation the rich provided funding for certain special public needs. The main liturgies were the *chorēgia*, in which a sponsor (*chorēgos*) supervised and paid for the training and performance of a chorus which sang and danced at a public festival,[22] and the trierarchy, in which a sponsor (trierarch) paid to equip and usually commanded a trireme, or warship, for a year. Some of these liturgies required substantial expenditures, but even so, some men spent far more than required in order to promote themselves and their public careers, and litigants often try to impress the jurors by referring to liturgies they have undertaken (see, e.g., Lys. 21.1–5). A further twist on this system was that if a man thought he had been assigned a liturgy that should have gone to someone else who was richer than he, he could propose an exchange of property (*antidosis*), giving the other man a choice of either taking over the liturgy or exchanging property with him. Finally, the rich were also subject to special taxes (*eisphorai*) levied as a percentage of their property in times of need.

The Athenian legal system remained similarly resistant to professionalization. Trials and the procedures leading up to them were supervised by officials, primarily the nine Archons, but their role was purely administrative, and they were in no way equivalent to modern judges. All significant questions about what we would call points of law were presented to the jurors, who considered them together with all other issues when they delivered their verdict at the end of the trial.[23] Trials were "contests" (*agōnes*) between two litigants, each of

---

[22] These included the productions of tragedy and comedy, for which the main expense was for the chorus.

[23] Certain religious "interpreters" (*exēgētai*) were occasionally asked to give their opinion on a legal matter that had a religious dimension (such as the prosecution of a homicide), but although these opinions could be reported in court

whom presented his own case to the jurors in a speech, plaintiff first, then defendant; in some cases each party then spoke again, probably in rebuttal. Since a litigant had only one or two speeches in which to present his entire case, and no issue was decided separately by a judge, all the necessary factual information and every important argument on substance or procedure, fact or law, had to be presented together. A single speech might thus combine narrative, argument, emotional appeal, and various digressions, all with the goal of obtaining a favorable verdict. Even more than today, a litigant's primary task was to control the issue—to determine which issues the jurors would consider most important and which questions they would have in their minds as they cast their votes. We only rarely have both speeches from a trial,[24] and we usually have little or no external evidence for the facts of a case or the verdict. We must thus infer both the facts and the opponent's strategy from the speech we have, and any assessment of the overall effectiveness of a speech and of the logographer's strategy is to some extent speculative.

Before a trial there were usually several preliminary hearings for presenting evidence; arbitration, public and private, was available and sometimes required. These hearings and arbitration sessions allowed each side to become familiar with the other side's case, so that discussions of "what my opponent will say" could be included in one's speech. Normally a litigant presented his own case, but he was often assisted by family or friends. If he wished (and could afford it), he could enlist the services of a logographer, who presumably gave strategic advice in addition to writing a speech. The speeches were timed to ensure an equal hearing for both sides,[25] and all trials were completed within a day. Two hundred or more jurors decided each case in the popular courts, which met in the Agora.[26] Homicide cases and

---

(e.g., Dem. 47.68–73), they had no official legal standing. The most significant administrative decision we hear of is the refusal of the Basileus to accept the case in Antiphon 6 (see 6.37–46).

[24] The exceptions are Demosthenes 19 and Aeschines 2, Aeschines 3 and Demosthenes 18, and Lysias 6 (one of several prosecution speeches) and Andocides 1; all were written for major public cases.

[25] Timing was done by means of a water-clock, which in most cases was stopped during the reading of documents.

[26] See Boegehold 1995.

certain other religious trials (e.g., Lys. 7) were heard by the Council of the Areopagus or an associated group of fifty-one Ephetae. The Areopagus was composed of all former Archons—perhaps 150–200 members at most times. It met on a hill called the Areopagus ("rock of Ares") near the Acropolis.

Jurors for the regular courts were selected by lot from those citizens who registered each year and who appeared for duty that day; as with the Assembly, a small payment allowed the poor to serve. After the speakers had finished, the jurors voted immediately without any formal discussion. The side with the majority won; a tie vote decided the case for the defendant. In some cases where the penalty was not fixed, after a conviction the jurors voted again on the penalty, choosing between penalties proposed by each side. Even when we know the verdict, we cannot know which of the speaker's arguments contributed most to his success or failure. However, a logographer could probably learn from jurors which points had or had not been successful, so that arguments that are found repeatedly in speeches probably were known to be effective in most cases.

The first written laws in Athens were enacted by Draco (ca. 620) and Solon (ca. 590), and new laws were regularly added. At the end of the fifth century the existing laws were reorganized, and a new procedure for enacting laws was instituted; thereafter a group of Law-Givers (*nomothetai*) had to certify that a proposed law did not conflict with any existing laws. There was no attempt, however, to organize legislation systematically, and although Plato, Aristotle, and other philosophers wrote various works on law and law-giving, these were either theoretical or descriptive and had no apparent influence on legislation. Written statutes generally used ordinary language rather than precise legal definitions in designating offenses, and questions concerning precisely what constituted a specific offense or what was the correct interpretation of a written statute were decided (together with other issues) by the jurors in each case. A litigant might, of course, assert a certain definition or interpretation as "something you all know" or "what the lawgiver intended," but such remarks are evidently tendentious and cannot be taken as authoritative.

The result of these procedural and substantive features was that the verdict depended largely on each litigant's speech (or speeches). As one speaker puts it (Ant. 6.18), "When there are no witnesses, you (jurors) are forced to reach a verdict about the case on the basis of the prose-

cutor's and defendant's words alone; you must be suspicious and examine their accounts in detail, and your vote will necessarily be cast
on the basis of likelihood rather than clear knowledge." Even the testimony of witnesses (usually on both sides) is rarely decisive. On the
other hand, most speakers make a considerable effort to establish facts
and provide legitimate arguments in conformity with established law.
Plato's view of rhetoric as a clever technique for persuading an ignorant crowd that the false is true is not borne out by the speeches, and
the legal system does not appear to have produced many arbitrary or
clearly unjust results.

The main form of legal procedure was a *dikē* ("suit") in which
the injured party (or his relatives in a case of homicide) brought suit
against the offender. Suits for injuries to slaves would be brought by
the slave's master, and injuries to women would be prosecuted by a
male relative. Strictly speaking, a *dikē* was a private matter between
individuals, though like all cases, *dikai* often had public dimensions.
The other major form of procedure was a *graphē* ("writing" or "indictment") in which "anyone who wished" (i.e., any citizen) could bring a
prosecution for wrongdoing. *Graphai* were instituted by Solon, probably in order to allow prosecution of offenses where the victim was
unable or unlikely to bring suit himself, such as selling a dependent
into slavery; but the number of areas covered by *graphai* increased to
cover many types of public offenses as well as some apparently private
crimes, such as *hybris*.

The system of prosecution by "anyone who wished" also extended
to several other more specialized forms of prosecution, like *eisangelia*
("impeachment"), used in cases of treason. Another specialized prosecution was *apagōgē* ("summary arrest"), in which someone could arrest
a common criminal (*kakourgos*, lit. "evil-doer"), or have him arrested,
on the spot. The reliance on private initiative meant that Athenians
never developed a system of public prosecution; rather, they presumed
that everyone would keep an eye on the behavior of his political enemies and bring suit as soon as he suspected a crime, both to harm his
opponents and to advance his own career. In this way all public officials would be watched by someone. There was no disgrace in admit-
ting that a prosecution was motivated by private enmity.

By the end of the fifth century the system of prosecution by "any
one who wished" was apparently being abused by so-called sykophants

(*sykophantai*), who allegedly brought or threatened to bring false suits against rich men, either to gain part of the fine that would be levied or to induce an out-of-court settlement in which the accused would pay to have the matter dropped. We cannot gauge the true extent of this problem, since speakers usually provide little evidence to support their claims that their opponents are sykophants, but the Athenians did make sykophancy a crime. They also specified that in many public procedures a plaintiff who either dropped the case or failed to obtain one-fifth of the votes would have to pay a heavy fine of 1,000 drachmas. Despite this, it appears that litigation was common in Athens and was seen by some as excessive.

Over the course of time, the Athenian legal and political systems have more often been judged negatively than positively. Philosophers and political theorists have generally followed the lead of Plato (427–347), who lived and worked in Athens his entire life while severely criticizing its system of government as well as many other aspects of its culture. For Plato, democracy amounted to the tyranny of the masses over the educated elite and was destined to collapse from its own instability. The legal system was capricious and depended entirely on the rhetorical ability of litigants with no regard for truth or justice. These criticisms have often been echoed by modern scholars, who particularly complain that law was much too closely interwoven with politics and did not have the autonomous status it achieved in Roman law and continues to have, at least in theory, in modern legal systems.

Plato's judgments are valid if one accepts the underlying presuppositions, that the aim of law is absolute truth and abstract justice and that achieving the highest good of the state requires thorough and systematic organization. Most Athenians do not seem to have subscribed to either the criticisms or the presuppositions, and most scholars now accept the long-ignored fact that despite major external disruptions in the form of wars and two short-lived coups brought about by one of these wars, the Athenian legal and political systems remained remarkably stable for almost two hundred years (508–320). Moreover, like all other Greek cities at the time, whatever their form of government, Athenian democracy was brought to an end not by internal forces but by the external power of Philip of Macedon and his son Alexander. The legal system never became autonomous, and the rich sometimes complained that they were victims of unscrupulous litigants, but there is no indication that the people wanted to yield control of the legal process to a professional class, as Plato recommended. For most Athenians—Plato being an exception in this and many other matters—one purpose of the legal system was to give everyone the opportunity to have his case heard by other citizens and have it heard quickly and cheaply; and in this it clearly succeeded.

Indeed, the Athenian legal system also served the interests of the rich, even the very rich, as well as the common people, in that it provided a forum for the competition that since Homer had been an important part of aristocratic life. In this competition, the rich used the courts as battlegrounds, though their main weapon was the rhetoric of popular ideology, which hailed the rule of law and promoted the ideal of moderation and restraint.[27] But those who aspired to political leadership and the honor and status that accompanied it repeatedly entered the legal arena, bringing suit against their political enemies whenever possible and defending themselves against suits brought by others whenever necessary. The ultimate judges of these public competitions were the common people, who seem to have relished the dramatic clash of individuals and ideologies. In this respect fourth-century oratory was the cultural heir of fifth-century drama and was similarly appreciated by the citizens. Despite the disapproval of intellectuals like Plato, most Athenians legitimately considered their legal system a hallmark of their democracy and a vital presence in their culture.

THE TRANSLATION OF GREEK ORATORY

The purpose of this series is to provide students and scholars in all fields with accurate, readable translations of all surviving classical Attic oratory, including speeches whose authenticity is disputed, as well as the substantial surviving fragments. In keeping with the originals, the language is for the most part nontechnical. Names of persons and places are given in the (generally more familiar) Latinized forms, and names of officials or legal procedures have been translated into English equivalents, where possible. Notes are intended to provide the necessary historical and cultural background; scholarly controversies are

---

[27] Ober 1989 is fundamental; see also Cohen 1995.

generally not discussed. The notes and introductions refer to scholarly treatments in addition to those listed below, which the reader may consult for further information.

Cross-references to other speeches follow the standard numbering system, which is now well established except in the case of Hyperides (for whom the numbering of the Oxford Classical Text is used).[28] References are by work and section (e.g., Dem. 24.73); spurious works are not specially marked; when no author is named (e.g., 24.73), the reference is to the same author as the annotated passage.

ABBREVIATIONS:

Aes.	=	Aeschines
And.	=	Andocides
Ant.	=	Antiphon
Arist.	=	Aristotle
Ath. Pol.	=	*The Athenian Constitution*
Dem.	=	Demosthenes
Din.	=	Dinarchus
Hyp.	=	Hyperides
Is.	=	Isaeus
Isoc.	=	Isocrates
Lyc.	=	Lycurgus
Lys.	=	Lysias
Plut.	=	Plutarch
Thuc.	=	Thucydides
Xen.	=	Xenophon

NOTE: The main unit of Athenian currency was the drachma; this was divided into obols and larger amounts were designated minas and talents.

1 drachma	=	6 obols
1 mina	=	100 drachmas
1 talent	=	60 minas (6,000 drachmas)

---

[28] For a listing of all the orators and their works, with classifications (forensic, deliberative, epideictic) and rough dates, see Edwards 1994: 74–79.

It is impossible to give an accurate equivalence in terms of modern currency, but it may be helpful to remember that the daily wage of some skilled workers was a drachma in the mid-fifth century and 2–2½ drachmas in the later fourth century. Thus it may not be too misleading to think of a drachma as worth about $50 or £33 and a talent as about $300,000 or £200,000 in 1997 currency.

BIBLIOGRAPHY OF WORKS CITED

Boegehold, Alan L., 1995: *The Lawcourts at Athens: Sites, Buildings, Equipment, Procedure, and Testimonia*. Princeton.

Bonner, Robert J., 1927: *Lawyers and Litigants in Ancient Athens*. Chicago.

Cohen, David, 1995: *Law, Violence and Community in Classical Athens*. Cambridge.

Cole, Thomas, 1991: *The Origins of Rhetoric in Ancient Greece*. Baltimore.

Dover, Kenneth J., 1968: *Lysias and the Corpus Lysiacum*. Berkeley.

———, 1974: *Greek Popular Morality in the Time of Plato and Aristotle*. Oxford.

———, 1978: *Greek Homosexuality*. London.

———, 1994: *Marginal Comment*. London.

Edwards, Michael, 1994: *The Attic Orators*. London.

Gagarin, Michael, and Paul Woodruff, 1995: *Early Greek Political Thought from Homer to the Sophists*. Cambridge.

Hansen, Mogens Herman, 1991: *The Athenian Democracy in the Age of Demosthenes*. Oxford.

Jebb, Richard, 1875: *The Attic Orators*, 2 vols. London.

Kennedy, George A., 1963: *The Art of Persuasion in Greece*. Princeton.

Kerferd, G. B., 1981: *The Sophistic Movement*. Cambridge.

MacDowell, Douglas M., 1978: *The Law in Classical Athens*. London.

———, ed. 1990: *Demosthenes, Against Meidias*. Oxford.

Ober, Josiah, 1989: *Mass and Elite in Democratic Athens*. Princeton.

Rhodes, P. J., trans., 1984: *Aristotle, The Athenian Constitution*. Penguin Books.

Sinclair, R. K., 1988: *Democracy and Participation in Athens*. Cambridge.

Todd, Stephen, 1993: *The Shape of Athenian Law*. Oxford.

Trevett, Jeremy, 1992: *Apollodoros the Son of Pasion*. Oxford.

————, 1996: "Did Demosthenes Publish His Deliberative Speeches?" *Hermes* 124: 425–441.

Usher, Stephen, 1976: "Lysias and His Clients," *Greek, Roman and Byzantine Studies* 17: 31–40.

————, trans., 1974–1985: *Dionysius of Halicarnassus, Critical Essays*. 2 vols. Loeb Classical Library. Cambridge, MA.

Wooten, Cecil W., trans., 1987: *Hermogenes' On Types of Style*. Chapel Hill, NC.

Worthington, Ian, 1994: "The Canon of the Ten Attic Orators," in *Persuasion: Greek Rhetoric in Action*, ed. Ian Worthington. London: 244–263.

Yunis, Harvey, 1996: *Taming Democracy: Models of Political Rhetoric in Classical Athens*. Ithaca, NY.

ANTIPHON

〰〰〰〰〰〰〰〰〰〰〰〰〰〰〰〰〰〰〰〰〰〰〰〰〰〰〰〰〰〰〰

Translated with introduction by Michael Gagarin

INTODUCTION

〰〰〰〰〰〰〰〰〰〰〰〰〰〰〰〰〰〰〰〰〰〰〰〰〰〰〰〰〰〰〰〰〰〰〰〰〰〰

Antiphon of Rhamnus (a deme, or precinct, in northern Attica) came from an old Athenian family.[1] Born around 480, he achieved enough prominence in the city to rate occasional mention by the comic poets, but for the most part he avoided public life. In 411, however, he was apparently one of the leaders of a group of aristocrats who staged a coup, replacing the democratic government with a ruling council of 400. This new government soon collapsed, and almost all its leaders went into exile, but Antiphon remained in Athens and was tried, convicted, and executed for treason. In his description of these events, Thucydides—who is reported to have been a pupil of Antiphon—gives him an exceptionally favorable notice (8.68):

> Of all the Athenians of his day Antiphon was a man of the most outstanding character (*aretē*) and had the greatest power of thought and expression. He did not come forward in public or willingly enter any dispute, being regarded with suspicion by the multitude because of his reputation for cleverness. Nevertheless, for those involved in a dispute, whether legal or political, he alone was most able to help whoever consulted him for advice.

Concerning Antiphon's trial for his role in the revolution, Thucydides adds, "Of all the men up to my time . . . he seems to me to have

---

[1] For a fuller treatment of these matters, with additional bibliography, see M. Gagarin, ed., *Antiphon, The Speeches* (Cambridge, 1997).

made the best defense in a capital case." Fragments of his lost speeches suggest that Antiphon traveled and had connections abroad, and his interest in public affairs is clear from the prominence of his clients or opponents, including Alcibiades and the general Demosthenes.

Later sources tell us that Antiphon taught others and that he was the first person to write speeches. Earlier orators, such as Themistocles or Pericles, delivered their own speeches and had no need of a written text, but around 430 Antiphon, who did not speak in public himself but advised others who would be speaking in court, began the practice of "logography"—the writing out of an entire speech for a friend or client to memorize and deliver as his own. Thus Attic oratory as we know it came into being. However, his interest in law and legal oratory developed earlier, and the three Tetralogies (each with two pairs of opposing speeches written for fictitious cases) may have been composed in the 430s, if not earlier.

The most disputed question about Antiphon's life is whether the orator is the same person as the author of two "sophistic" treatises, *On Truth* and *On Concord*, that were assigned to him in antiquity, or whether there was at the time another Antiphon, a sophist, who is portrayed in Xenophon's *Memorabilia* 1.6.[2] There were many Antiphons in antiquity, and ancient scholars often confused them, though most apparently considered the orator who wrote the speeches in this volume to be the same person as the Antiphon who wrote sophistic treatises. The separatist position gained strength early in this century with the discovery of several papyrus fragments of *On Truth*, in which the author seems to present an egalitarian view of society and to advocate obedience to the requirements of nature (*physis*) as against the rules of law and custom (*nomos*). Some scholars found it inconceivable that this "anarchist" could be the same man as the aristocrat who in his speeches repeatedly expresses respect for the laws. More recently, however, the unitarian position has gained ground; scholars now recognize

---

[2] Recent treatments of the question of identity can be found in Harry C. Avery, "One Antiphon or Two?" *Hermes* 110 (1982): 145–158, and Gerard Pendrick, "Once again Antiphon the Sophist and Antiphon of Rhamnus," *Hermes* 115 (1987): 47–60.

that an orator who praises the law in a client's speech before a jury is not necessarily voicing his own opinion, and the papyrus fragments are less often understood as a call to anarchy; moreover, a new papyrus fragment has forced a revision of part of the text of *On Truth*, eliminating an earlier reconstruction in which the author appeared to challenge the traditional class structure. Scholars now also recognize that stylistic differences between different works composed for different purposes and different audiences—some perhaps for a reading audience, others for oral delivery—cannot be used as evidence for separate authorship. Most compelling, however, is Thucydides' picture of Antiphon of Rhamnus (quoted above), which could serve as the description of a typical sophist: a leading intellectual, whose special talent was writing speeches for others and who had a reputation for cleverness, especially with words. There is so much overlap between what we know of the "sophist" and the "orator" that without much stronger evidence to the contrary, we should conclude that they are one and the same.

On this reading Antiphon was a leading Athenian intellectual interested in many different issues of his day from geometry (he proposed a method for squaring the circle) to rhetoric, whose special interest was law and justice. A friend of the rich and powerful, he avoided speaking in public but advised friends on legal matters, ultimately creating the new profession of logography. Combining a quick intellect with rhetorical skill and a thorough knowledge of the law, he earned large sums.[3] But however successful he may have been for his clients, he lost his final case—the only speech he delivered in his own behalf (Ant. Fr. 1).

We do not know how many speeches Antiphon wrote or "published" (made available for copying and distribution to others) during his career. By the first century BC some sixty works were attributed to Antiphon, some of which ancient scholars judged spurious. The speeches were arranged by subject matter, the speeches for homicide cases coming first. The six complete works we have today are from this group; they probably survived because they were the first six in the

---

[3] See note on Antiphon Fragment 1a.

ancient corpus. Three of these (1, 5, 6) were written for actual trials and are generally accepted as authentic. The manuscripts also preserve three Tetralogies (2, 3, 4),[4] and we have titles and fragments of twenty other works, including Antiphon's final speech "On the Revolution" (Fr. 1). Later writers also credit Antiphon with an *Art of Rhetoric* and a collection of *Prologues*, though some scholars doubt the authenticity of these, and we have fragments from three "sophistic" works: *On Truth*, *On Concord*, and *Politicus*.[5]

Since the end of the nineteenth century the authenticity of the Tetralogies has been disputed by scholars who argue that historical, legal, and stylistic discrepancies set them apart from the three court speeches.[6] But many of these alleged discrepancies can be explained if we keep in mind that these works were probably intended to be read, studied, and discussed by others. If genuine, they are probably early works of Antiphon, perhaps as early as the 440s, and thus among the earliest examples we have of Attic prose, which soon superseded Ionic prose as the medium of intellectual communication throughout the Greek world. Their influence on the style of Thucydides, the first great master of Attic prose, is evident. And the arguments of the Tetralogies fit well with the intellectual interests of the second half of the fifth century BC and the spirit of experimentation characteristic of the sophists. In particular, arguments based on likelihood (*eikos*) in the First Tetralogy and the nexus of arguments concerning cause, effect, blame, and responsibility in the Second and Third can be paralleled in the work of the earliest writers on rhetoric, Corax, Tisias, and Gorgias. It is always difficult to prove authenticity, but there is no good reason not to accept the traditional ascription of the Tetralogies to Antiphon. These works demonstrate well the powers of thinking

---

[4] It is confusing that the numbering of the Tetralogies and the corpus differ; all references in this work are to corpus numbers (e.g., Ant. 3 = Second Tetralogy).

[5] All the fragments of Antiphon together with the complete works are translated by J. S. Morrison, "Antiphon" in *The Older Sophists*, ed. Rosamond K. Sprague (Columbia, SC, 1972): 106–240.

[6] The best presentation of the arguments is R. Sealey, "The *Tetralogies* Ascribed to Antiphon," *Transactions of the American Philological Association* 114 (1984): 71–85.

and speaking that Thucydides praised in Antiphon (8.68), as well as the cleverness that aroused popular suspicion against him.

Antiphon's great strength as a logographer is argumentation, the selection, composition, and arrangement of arguments in such a way as to make the best possible case for a client. He may lack the clarity of exposition of Lysias or the emotional appeal of Demosthenes, and he shows relatively little interest in the development of his speaker's character (*ēthos*); but the accumulation of different kinds of argument in his speeches produces a powerful effect. A hallmark of Antiphon's argumentation is its flexibility. The traditional four-part division of a speech into prologue, narrative, proof or argument, and epilogue was said to have been devised by Tisias a generation earlier, but Antiphon often follows these divisions only loosely, fitting his presentation to the needs of the case. Thus the narrative in Antiphon 1 is more detailed and relatively much longer than in 5 or 6, in part because 1 is a speech for the prosecution and thus needs to present the first account of the facts to the jurors, but also because the speaker lacks the evidence that might support other arguments. Antiphon sometimes blurs the line between the different parts of a speech, moreover, so that even where he moves explicitly from the facts to the argument, as at 5.25, he in fact continues to present a mixture of both with only a shift in emphasis.

These considerations do not apply to the Tetralogies, which must be approached differently. Since Antiphon controls the speeches on both sides, we must assume that every relevant fact or argument is included in the text. The legal context is generally consistent with Athenian law, but the Tetralogies pay little attention to the details of actual laws, which may be distorted or ignored. Moreover, since these are not actual cases but examples of forensic argument, the facts are kept to a minimum, so that the entire emphasis can be put on argumentation. For the sake of clarity, arguments are often matched point-for-point with counter-arguments in a way that was undoubtedly rare in actual cases. Thus, the reader of the Tetralogies should not ask what are the facts or where does the truth lie, but how valid (or perhaps how interesting) are the arguments and what can we learn from them.

The following translations are based on my recent Greek text (above, n. 1), which also has an introduction, a commentary, and a bibliography. Greekless readers can find more material about Antiphon in Morrison's more complete translation (above, n. 5); he includes ancient testimonia to the life and work of Antiphon, as well as all the fragments.

1. AGAINST THE STEPMOTHER

〰〰〰

This speech is delivered by a young man who is prosecuting his stepmother for poisoning his father. She is defended by her son, his half-brother. The death occurred some time ago, when the speaker was a boy (1.30); he may only recently have turned eighteen, the minimum age for bringing a legal case.

The "facts" are set forth in a vivid narrative (1.14–20), whose details must have come partly, perhaps largely, from the speaker's imagination. There is no real evidence and little argument other than the allegation of an earlier attempt at a similar poisoning. Modern scholars have tended to accept the analysis of a similar (the same?) case in the Aristotelian treatise *Magna Moralia* (1188b29–38), where a woman accused of poisoning her husband is acquitted because her intent was to secure his love, not to kill him; but the speaker pays relatively little attention to this consideration. Rather, he emphasizes his own loyalty and his brother's and stepmother's corresponding disloyalty to his father, drawing parallels with the story of Clytemnestra (1.17), who treacherously killed her husband Agamemnon and was in turn killed by their son Orestes (see Aeschylus' *Oresteia* trilogy). The appeal to stereotypical behavior of women as a continual threat to men—plotting, using drugs, concerned primarily with love—may have been more effective with the male jurors than the defense's presumed response that she acted out of love. Even if the defense argued persuasively that the intent was not to kill, the jurors may have concluded that her behavior was nonetheless so threatening to the stability of the family that she deserved punishment.

The case was tried before the court of the Areopagus (see Series Introduction). As usual, we do not know the verdict and know nothing of the defense's arguments beyond what we can surmise from this speech. The date is unknown but is usually placed in the period 420–411.

1.

[1] I am still so young and inexperienced in legal matters,[1] gentlemen, that I face a terrible dilemma in this case: either I fail in my duty to my father, who instructed me to prosecute his murderers, or, if I do prosecute, I am forced to quarrel with people who should least of all be my opponents—my own half-brothers and these brothers' mother. [2] But fortune and these opponents themselves have forced me to bring this case. It would be more reasonable for them to seek vengeance for the dead man and assist my prosecution, but they did just the opposite: they opposed my suit and are thus murderers themselves, as I and my indictment both state. [3] If I show that their mother murdered our father intentionally and with premeditation, and indeed that she was caught in the act of contriving his death not just once but many times before, then I beg you, gentlemen, take vengeance, first for your laws, which you received from the gods and your ancestors, for you convict people by these laws just as they did; second, take vengeance for the dead man, and at the same time help me who am left all alone. [4] You are now my family while they, who ought to avenge the dead man and help me, have become his murderers and my opponents. Where can one turn for help? Where can one take refuge except with you and with justice?

[5] I am amazed at my brother. What is he thinking in opposing my case? Does he think piety consists simply in not forsaking his mother? Well, I think it is much more of a sacrilege to abandon vengeance for the dead man, especially since he died as the involuntary victim of a plot, whereas she killed with full intention and foreknowl-

---

[1] The plea of inexperience becomes a rhetorical *topos* ("commonplace"), though as P. J. Rhodes well observes (*Greece & Rome* 41 [1994]: 158), "the fact that a passage is a *topos*, that it says what is conventionally said in a particular situation, and perhaps expresses it in a conventional way, does not exclude the possibility that it is an authentic report, or that what is stated is true."

edge. [6] How can he say he is "quite certain"² that his mother did not kill our father? When he had the opportunity to gain certain knowledge through an interrogation of slaves,³ he refused, but he was eager to try methods that could not produce information. However, he should have been eager for the proposal I made in my challenge, so that the truth of the matter could be fully examined. [7] If the slaves did not agree with me, he could have eagerly defended himself against me with certainty, and his mother would be entirely free of the charge. But since he was unwilling to put the facts to a test, how can he know things he wasn't willing to investigate? Surely then, jurors, it isn't likely that he knows things when he didn't accept the truth about them. [8] What defense will he make? Since he was quite certain he couldn't save her by interrogating the slaves, he thought safety might lie in avoiding an interrogation; that way, he thought, the facts might disappear. How then can he have truly sworn an oath that he is "quite certain," when I wanted to carry out a completely fair interrogation, but he was unwilling to obtain certain knowledge about the matter? [9] I wanted to interrogate their slaves, for they knew that on a previous occasion this woman—the mother of these men—had contrived our father's death by poisoning, that he had caught her in the act, and that she had not denied it, except to claim she was giving the drug as a love potion, not to kill him. [10] I therefore wanted to conduct an interrogation about these facts as follows.⁴ I wrote down the accusa-

---

²The speaker is probably quoting directly from the defendant's preliminary oath affirming the woman's innocence.

³In theory, the interrogation of slaves under torture (*basanos*) was the only means of introducing the testimony of slaves in court. The interrogation is regularly proposed in a challenge, issued by one litigant to the other. We know of no cases, however, where a challenge actually resulted in an interrogation. In practice, the challenge is rejected by the other litigant, providing the challenger with the rhetorical opportunity (as here) to tell the jurors what the slaves would have said had they been interrogated (see M. Gagarin, "The Torture of Slaves in Athenian Law," *Classical Philology* 91 [1996]: 1–18). In criminal investigations an interrogation could take place without a challenge (see Ant. 5.29–42).

⁴The speaker's conduct, as he presents it, conforms to the proper rules of the challenge: the challenger determines (and here writes down) the questions to be asked, which generally require simple, yes-or-no answers.

tion I was making against the woman and asked these men to conduct the interrogation in my presence; this way the slaves would not be forced to say what I asked them, for I was satisfied if they used the written questions. I think I am justified in taking this as evidence that I was prosecuting my father's murderer justly and correctly. If the slaves should deny or disagree with my assertions, the interrogation would force the accusation to conform to the facts, for it forces even those who are prepared to lie to make true accusations. [11] Now I am quite certain that if they had approached me [5] the moment they heard the news that I was going to prosecute my father's murderer and had offered to hand over their slaves for interrogation and I had refused to accept them, they would be presenting this as the strongest possible evidence that they were innocent of the murder. So since I am the one who wanted to conduct the interrogation myself, at first, and then asked them to conduct it instead, it is only reasonable that these same considerations should be evidence for my side that they are guilty. [12] If they were willing to hand over slaves for interrogation and I had refused them, this would be evidence for their side. In the same way, then, consider it evidence for my side that they refused to hand over their slaves when I wanted to put the matter to the test. It seems to me a terrible thing if they are trying to persuade you not to convict them, when they did not see fit to become jurors in their own case by handing over their own slaves for interrogation. [13] In this matter, then, it is clear that they were trying to avoid a clear investigation of the facts; they knew that their own wickedness would become apparent, and so they wanted to let the matter rest in silence without an interrogation. But not you, gentlemen; I am quite certain you will make things clear. But enough about that. I will now try to give you a true account of what happened, and may justice be my guide.

[14] Our house had an upstairs room where Philoneus, a true gentleman and a friend of our father, used to stay when he was in Athens. Now, Philoneus had a mistress [6] whom he was going to set up as a prostitute. Learning of this, my brother's mother became friends with her. [15] She realized that Philoneus was treating the woman wrongly,

---

[5] This "hypothetical role-reversal" is common in Antiphon (5.38, 5.74, 5.84, 6.27, 6.28).

[6] The status of this woman is disputed, but she is probably a slave.

and so she summoned her and, when she arrived, said she too was being treated wrongly by our father. If the woman followed her instructions, she said, she was capable of renewing Philoneus' love for her and my father's love for herself. She added that her job was to contrive the plan, the woman's was to carry it out. [16] She asked the woman if she was willing to help, and she agreed—without hesitation, I think. Some time later it was time for Philoneus to attend to the sacrificial rites of Zeus Ctesius in Piraeus,[7] and since my father was about to sail for Naxos, Philoneus thought it would be an excellent idea to accompany his good friend, my father, to Piraeus and on the same trip entertain him after celebrating the rites. [17] Philoneus' mistress accompanied them to help with the sacrifice. When they reached Piraeus, Philoneus carried out the sacrifice in the proper manner. When he had finished, the woman began planning how she should give them the drug: should it be before or after dinner? Finally following the advice of Clytemnestra—this man's mother—she decided it would be better to give it after dinner. [18] It would take too long for me to tell and for you to hear the details of the dinner, but I will try to relate the rest of the story about the giving of the drug as briefly as possible. When they had finished dinner, seeing as one of them was celebrating a sacrifice to Zeus Ctesius and entertaining his guest while the other was preparing to sail and was dining with his friend, they naturally began pouring libations and adding frankincense to them. [19] But while Philoneus' mistress was pouring the libations, and the men were uttering prayers that would never be fulfilled, at the same time, gentlemen, she was pouring in the drug. And she also thought she would be clever and put more into Philoneus' cup, on the theory that if she gave him more, he would love her more. She didn't realize she had been deceived by my stepmother until the evil was already done. She gave my father a smaller amount. [20] When the men had poured out the libations, each took hold of his own murderer and drank it down—his last drink. Philoneus died immediately, and our father became sick and died from the illness twenty days later. For this deed the woman who assisted with it has the reward she deserves, even

---

[7] Zeus Ctesius ("god of property") was naturally honored by the wealthy. Philoneus is apparently a merchant residing in Piraeus, the port of Athens; he stays with the speaker's father when he is in the city.

though she was not to blame: she was tortured on the wheel and then handed over to the executioner.[8] And the woman who was really responsible and who thought up the plan and carried it out,[9] she will have her reward too, if you and the gods are willing.

[21] Consider now how much more just my request is than my brother's. I am asking you to avenge this man's wrongful death for all time; he asks for nothing for the dead man, though he deserves your pity and help and revenge for the impious and infamous way he departed this life before his appointed time, victim of those who should least of all have done this. [22] Instead, he will make requests for the killer that are immoral, unholy, impossible, and unworthy of consideration by you or the gods; for he asks you not to punish her for a crime she could not persuade herself to avoid. You are here not to assist murderers but their victims who have been intentionally killed—killed by those who should least of all have killed them. So now it is in your hands to decide this case correctly. Be sure to do so. [23] My opponent will plead for his mother, who is still living despite her thoughtless and godless act of murder, and will try to persuade you that she should not pay the penalty for her crime. But I plead for my father, who is dead, that she should pay the penalty to the fullest. And your task, the reason you are jurors and have that name,[10] is to bring criminals to justice. [24] I am prosecuting her with this speech so that she will pay the penalty for her crime and I will gain revenge for our father and for your laws, and I deserve help from all of you if I speak the truth. He is doing just the opposite, helping her escape punishment for her crime, even though she disregarded the laws. [25] Does justice require punishment for a person who kills intentionally or not? Who should we pity more, the dead man or the killer?

---

[8] The torture was probably punitive, since if the woman had also been interrogated under torture, the speaker would probably report what she said. Her involvement in the death was great enough to justify her punishment even if she was not the main instigator.

[9] Strictly speaking, the servant carried out the crime, and many editors move the words "and carried it out" to the preceding sentence. But since the speaker's strategy is to shift all the responsibility to the stepmother, he would want to exaggerate her role.

[10] "Juror" (*dikastēs*) is derived from "justice" (*dikē*).

The dead man, in my view, since that would be in accord with justice and righteousness, both human and divine. So again I ask you: just as she showed no pity and no mercy in killing him, so she should herself be put to death by you and by justice. [26] She killed him willingly and with premeditation; he died unwillingly and violently. Surely, gentlemen, he did die violently.[11] He was about to sail abroad and was being entertained by one of his friends; she sent the poison and gave orders that it be given to him to drink, thus killing our father. How could she deserve any pity or respect from you or anyone else, when she herself didn't think to show pity for her own husband but destroyed him without shame or respect? [27] You know it's right to show pity for involuntary suffering rather than for willing and intentional crimes and errors. Just as she destroyed him, with no respect and no fear for gods or heroes or humans, so she would receive the just punishment she most deserves if she is put to death by you and by justice, without respect or pity or sympathy.

[28] I am amazed at my brother's audacity. He swears he is "quite certain" that his mother did not do these things; but how could someone be quite certain of something that happened when he wasn't there himself? Surely those who plot the murder of their close friends and relatives do not contrive their schemes and make their preparations in front of witnesses but in the greatest possible secrecy so that no one else will know. [29] The victims of plots know nothing until the evil is already done and they understand the destruction that has come on them. Then, if they can and have enough time before their death, they summon their friends or relatives as witnesses, tell them who is causing their death, and direct them to take vengeance for the wrongs they are suffering. [30] This is just how my father directed me, though I was just a boy, when he was suffering his terrible last illness. If victims lack

---

[11] The prosecution may have a problem because the law on homicide (see Dem. 23.22) treats poisoning as murder "if one gives the poison oneself," implying perhaps that someone who only supplied the poison is not guilty of homicide. By asserting that his father died a "violent death" (though nothing indicates that it actually was violent), the speaker may be trying to present this as an ordinary case of murder, and not just a poisoning. In ordinary homicide, an accomplice (the "planner") was considered just as responsible as the actual killer (see Introduction to Ant. 6).

these means, they write things down, and they summon their own servants as witnesses and reveal to them who is causing their death. Young as I was at the time, my father revealed these matters to me and gave instructions to me, not his slaves.

[31] I have told my story and have come to the help of the dead man and the law. It is up to you by yourselves to consider what remains to be done and decide in accordance with justice. The gods below, I think, are concerned about the victims of crime.

THE TETRALOGIES

〜〜

The three Tetralogies[1] are artificial exercises in the form of speeches to an Athenian court (where each litigant in a private case would give two speeches). They illustrate different types of argument. In the first the facts are in dispute: did the accused do it? In the second the facts are admitted, but the legal consequences of those facts are in dispute: should the defendant be held legally responsible for the boy's death? In the third several issues are raised, but the main dispute concerns justification: does the defendant's claim of self-defense justify his actions? The apparent aim of these exercises is to provide examples of legal argumentation that would provide useful training for the variety of cases a litigant might face (not just homicide). As such, they share certain features: narratives are omitted or reduced to the bare essentials necessary to understand the case, and no witnesses are called to testify. Primary attention is given to the arguments, which become rather complex, especially as argument is answered by counter-argument, which is then answered in turn.

The issue of pollution for homicide is prominent in the prologues and epilogues of all three Tetralogies. Both sides argue that a killer is polluted and his pollution also pollutes the whole city. Both sides claim a religious duty to see that the true killer is tried and convicted. Convicting an innocent man or not convicting the true killer will bring pollution on whichever litigant errs and perhaps also on the jurors. If the killer goes free, moreover, the whole city will suffer: its

---

[1] On the question of the authenticity of the Tetralogies, see the Introduction to Antiphon above.

sanctuaries will be defiled and its crops ruined. Pollution is much less prominent, however, in Antiphon's other speeches (cf. 5.81–83) and does not seem to have been an important factor in actual Athenian homicide law.

Later rhetoricians placed the Tetralogies in their general classification of legal cases according to the "issue" (*stasis*; Latin *status*) raised by the case, the most basic division being (to oversimplify) between questions of fact and questions of law—such as whether the facts constitute an offense, whether the act was otherwise justified, and so forth.[2]

---

[2] See further Kennedy 1963: 306–314.

2. FIRST TETRALOGY

A man and his servant have been killed in the street late at night. When the crime was discovered, the man was already dead, but the servant, before dying, apparently identified the accused as the murderer. This direct evidence is disputed (the servant would be biased), and additional arguments are elaborated, most of which take the form of arguments from likelihood or probability (*eikos*): no one else is likely to have killed the man; or, the accused had a strong motive; or, his previous dealings with the victim made him more likely to avoid killing him. This type of argument was especially favored by the two figures traditionally credited with inventing rhetoric, Corax and Tisias.[1] Another commonplace argument is the citation of previous service to the city. Toward the end of his second speech (2.4.8) the defendant offers an alibi; if confirmed, this would provide strong evidence in his favor, probably strong enough to decide the case, but the issue is not developed.

2.1

[1] It is not difficult to obtain a conviction for crimes planned by ordinary people, but when those with natural ability and previous experience commit a crime at that point in their lives when their mental facilities are at their height, it is difficult to get any knowledge or proof of it. [2] Because of the great risk involved, in their planning they pay close attention to security and do not undertake anything without first guarding against all possible suspicion. You should be aware of this

---

[1] See Series Introduction.

and even if you accept a point as only likely (*eikos*), you should have confidence in it. For our part, in bringing this homicide case we are not letting the guilty one go free in order to prosecute an innocent man. [3] We know that the whole city is polluted by the killer until he is prosecuted and that if we prosecute the wrong man, we will be guilty of impiety, and punishment for any mistake you make (in convicting him) will fall on us. Since the entire pollution thus falls on us, we will try to show you as clearly as possible from the facts at our disposal that he killed the man.

[4] ⟨Common criminals² are not likely (*eikos*) to have killed the man,⟩ for no one who went so far as to risk his life would abandon the gain he had securely in hand; and yet the victims were still wearing their cloaks when they were found. The killer wasn't someone who was drunk, for he would have been identified by his fellow drinkers. He wasn't killed in a quarrel, for they were not quarreling in the middle of the night in a deserted place. And no one would have killed him by accident when aiming at someone else, for then his attendant wouldn't have been killed too. [5] So all other suspicions are removed, and the circumstances of the death show that it was deliberately planned. Who is more likely to have attacked him than someone who has already suffered great harm from him and expects to suffer even more? That person is the defendant, who is his old enemy and has prosecuted him many times on serious charges but never gained a conviction. [6] In turn he was prosecuted even more often and on more serious charges, and since he never once won acquittal, he has lost most of his property. Most recently the defendant was indicted by him for theft of sacred property with a penalty of two talents.³ He knew full well he was guilty, he knew his opponent's ability from previous experience, and he harbored resentment from the earlier incidents. In all likeli-

---

² The first part of this sentence is missing in the manuscripts of Antiphon, but words to this effect must have been there originally. "Common criminals" translates the Greek word *kakourgoi*, which occurs in the defendant's response to this argument (e.g., 2.4.5–6). *Kakourgoi* were subject to the procedure of *apagōgē* (see Series Introduction). Originally, *kakourgoi* designated common street criminals, such as thieves and muggers (cf. 5.9). The most serious street crime in Athens was *lopodusia* or the theft of a cloak, a cloak being normally the most valuable possession a man had with him in public.

³ Equivalent to perhaps $600,000; see Series Introduction.

hood, therefore, he formed this plan, and in all likelihood he killed the man to defend himself against this hostile action. [7] Desire for revenge made him unmindful of the danger, and fear of impending disaster fired him with greater eagerness to attempt the crime. He hoped by this action to kill the man without being caught and to be free from that indictment, since without a prosecutor the case would be dropped.[4] [8] Even if he should be caught, he thought it more honorable to gain his revenge and suffer the consequences than to be a coward and do nothing but let himself be destroyed by the impending prosecution. He was quite certain he would be convicted in that case; otherwise he would not have thought this trial offered him a better chance. [9] These considerations forced him to commit this unholy crime. As for witnesses, if many had been present, we would have presented many here. But since only his attendant was present, those who heard him speak will testify. For he was still breathing when we picked him up and questioned him, and he said he recognized this man alone among those who attacked them.

Since, then, his guilt is established both by arguments from likelihood and by those who were present, there is no way his acquittal could be just or advantageous. [10] For it would be impossible to convict those who plan crimes if they cannot be convicted either by the testimony of those present or by arguments from likelihood; and it is harmful to you if this polluted and unholy person should enter the precincts of the gods and pollute their holiness or share the tables of innocent men and infect them with this pollution. Acts such as these cause harvests to fail and affairs in general to miscarry. [11] So make this man's punishment your own concern: attribute his impiety to him alone, and you will insure that his misfortune remains his alone and the city remains untainted by it.

2.2

[1] I don't think I'm wrong to consider myself most unfortunate of all men. Others suffer misfortunes, but if their troubles are caused by

---

[4] Theft of sacred property was a public action (a *graphē*), so that any citizen who wished could prosecute (see Series Introduction). But such cases were often brought by the accused's political enemies, and the speaker reasons that with the defendant's main enemy dead, no one else would prosecute.

a storm, these cease when good weather returns; if they fall sick, the danger passes when they recover their health; and if some other misfortune assails them, a reversal of conditions brings relief. [2] But in my case, when this person was alive he was ruining me and my family, and now that he is dead, even if I am acquitted, he has caused me considerable pain and anxiety. For my bad luck has reached the point that showing my decency and innocence will not be enough to save me from ruin. Unless I can also find the true killer and prove his guilt—something they in their quest for revenge are unable to do—then I will be judged guilty of murder and wrongly convicted. [3] They claim that my cleverness makes it hard to establish my guilt, but they also accuse me of foolishness when they argue that my actions show that I did the deed. For if the enormous hostility between us leads you now to consider me the likely suspect, then it was even more likely that before committing the crime I would foresee that I was going to be the obvious suspect, and far from committing the murder myself and willingly incurring the obvious suspicion, I would even prevent others from killing him if I learned they were planning to do so.⁵ For if the deed itself showed that I was the killer,⁶ I was doomed, and even if I escaped detection, I was quite certain I would incur this suspicion. [4] I am thus in this miserable position: I am forced not only to defend myself but also to reveal the true killers. Still, I must try, for it seems that nothing is more bitter than necessity. I have no other way to proceed than with arguments the prosecutor used when he absolved others of the crime and claimed that the circumstances of the death show that I am the murderer. For if making them seem innocent makes the crime appear to be my doing, then it is only right that making them suspect should make me seem innocent.

[5] It is not unlikely, as they claim, but likely that someone wandering around in the middle of the night would be killed for his cloak. That his cloak was not removed proves nothing. If the killers didn't remove it in time but left it there because they were frightened by

---

⁵ This type of argument (see also 2.2.6) can be termed "reverse-*eikos*" (the fact that a person is likely to commit a crime in fact makes him unlikely to do so because he knows he will be the obvious suspect). It is attributed to both Corax (Aristotle, *Rhetoric* 2.24.11) and Tisias (Plato, *Phaedrus* 273a–c).

⁶ He probably means, "if I was caught in the act."

others approaching, then they were acting prudently; they were not crazy to prefer their own safety to considerations of profit. [6] If he wasn't killed for his cloak, perhaps he noticed others committing some crime and was killed so he wouldn't report it. Who knows? There are also many others who hated him almost as much as I did; surely one of these is more likely to have killed him. It was clear to them that I would be suspected, and I was quite certain I would be blamed instead of them. [7] As for the attendant's testimony, how can you believe it? Terrified by the danger, it is not likely that he recognized the killers, but it is likely he was persuaded to agree with his masters. Since the testimony of slaves in general is untrustworthy—otherwise we wouldn't torture them[7]—how can it be right for you to believe this witness' testimony and destroy me?

[8] If anyone thinks arguments from likelihood carry as much weight against me as the truth, by the same reasoning he should consider it more likely that in planning I would watch out for my own safety and would take care not to be present at the crime rather than let this man recognize me as he was being killed. [9] Unless I was out of my mind, I did not think this crime presented less danger than the indictment I was facing, but rather far more, as I will show. If I was convicted in that case, I knew I would lose my property, but I wouldn't lose my life or my city. I would survive, and even if I had to borrow money, I wouldn't have faced total destruction. But if I am convicted now and put to death, I shall leave a foul disgrace for my children; or if I go into exile, an old man without a country, I'll be a beggar in a foreign land. [10] Thus all their accusations are unconvincing. If it is likely but not a fact that I killed the man, then it is only just that I be acquitted. I was clearly defending myself against an enormous injustice; otherwise it wouldn't seem likely that I killed him. Your proper task, however, is to convict killers, not those who have a reason to kill.

[11] Since I am absolved of the charge in every way, I will not defile the holiness of the gods if I enter their sacred precincts, and I will not offend them if I persuade you to acquit me. But the prosecution, who charge me, an innocent man, but let the guilty one go free—they are the ones to blame for the failure of harvests. They urge you to offend

---

[7] 1.6n.

against the gods, and they should suffer all the punishment they say I deserve. [12] That's what they deserve, so don't believe their arguments. If you consider everything I have done, you will know that I didn't make plots or seek anything improper. On the contrary, I have contributed generously to many special levies, outfitted many triremes, produced splendid choral performances, loaned money to many friends, and guaranteed many large debts as well.[8] I have acquired my property, moreover, by hard work, not litigation;[9] I have performed sacrifices and obeyed the laws. That's the way I am, so don't convict me of anything unholy or disgraceful. [13] If the victim were still alive, I would not only be defending myself but would also show that he and his helpers have no concern for justice but are bringing this case only for their own profit. I pass over these matters out of decency rather than justice. So I implore you, gentlemen, since you judge and oversee the greatest matters, take pity on my misfortune and cure it. Do not join their attack and let them subject me to this lawless and godless destruction.

2.3

[1] He wrongs misfortune when he tries to use her to mask his crimes and remove his pollution. But he deserves no pity from you; he brought disaster on the unwilling victim but willingly got himself into this danger. In my earlier speech I showed that he killed the man; I will now try to refute the claims he made in his defense.

[2] If the killers had seen others approaching and had fled, leaving the victims there without removing their cloaks, then those who dis-

---

[8] Previous service to the city is often mentioned in court. Here the defendant claims to have undertaken every possible service as often as possible; in a real case the speaker would only mention appropriate services. The first three services are the common public "liturgies" (see Series Introduction): *eisphorai* are special wartime levies on the rich; a trierarch underwrites the cost of equipping and maintaining a trireme for a year; and a choregus or "producer" pays the expenses of training a chorus (see Ant. 6). The two services listed after these are common private ways of helping friends.

[9] I.e., he was not engaged in sykophancy (see Series Introduction; cf. 3.2.1n). On the contrary, he accuses his opponents of sykophancy (2.2.13), though he gives no proof.

covered the victims would have gotten a clear story from the servant, who was still conscious when they found him even if his master was already dead, and they would have reported the culprits to us so that this man would not be blamed. Or if others had been seen committing a crime and had killed the victims so that they wouldn't be identified, then the other crime would have been reported at the same time as this murder, and suspicion would have fallen on those others. [3] And I don't know how those who were in less danger would have plotted against him more readily than those who had more to fear. For the latter, fear and the great wrong they had suffered overcame their caution; whereas for the former, the danger and disgrace of the crime outweighed their dispute and moderated the vehemence of their spirit, if they even contemplated such action. [4] They are wrong to say you should not believe the attendant's evidence. For evidence like that we don't torture slaves, we free them. In cases where they deny a theft or conspire with their masters to conceal a crime, then we consider their testimony truthful only under torture. [5] And the accused is no more likely to have been absent than present: he would run the same risk absent as present, since anyone captured at the scene would have confirmed that he was the planner;[10] but the execution of the crime would have suffered, since none of his agents would be as eager for it as he. [6] I will also show that he thought the indictment posed not a smaller but a far greater risk than this trial. Let's assume he had the same expectation of conviction or acquittal in each case. He had no hope of avoiding trial on the indictment as long as this man was alive, for he would never agree to a settlement; but in this case he hoped to avoid trial, since he thought he could kill the man without being caught. [7] If he thinks you should not suspect him because he's the obvious suspect, he is wrong. If the risk of suspicion was enough to deter this man from attacking when he faced the gravest danger, then no one would have planned the murder; anyone in less danger would be even less likely than he to attempt the crime, since the fear of incurring suspicion would still outweigh the danger he was facing. [8] The special levies and choral productions are a good indication of his prosperity but not of his innocence. On the contrary, fear of los-

---

[10] For the "planner" of a homicide, see 4.2.5n and the Introduction to Antiphon 6.

ing this prosperity makes it likely that he committed this unholy murder. And when he says that murderers are not those who are likely to have killed but those who actually did kill, he is correct about those who killed, if it were clear to us who his actual killers were. But if the actual killers have not been revealed, then since his guilt is proven by the arguments from likelihood, this man and no other would be the killer; for such things are not done in the presence of witnesses but secretly.

[9] Since from his own defense it is clearly proven that he killed the man, his plea is nothing more than a request that you transfer his pollution onto yourselves.[11] We, on the other hand, ask for nothing; we simply tell you that if neither likelihood nor witnesses can convict this man, then no defendant can any longer be convicted. [10] If you acquit him wrongly, the dead man's spirit will not seek revenge from us but will weigh on your consciences. You know quite certainly how he died, you know that the tracks of suspicion lead to this man, and you have the attendant's reliable testimony; how in all justice can you acquit him? [11] With this in mind, assist the victim, punish the killer, and purify the city. You will achieve three good results: fewer men will plot crimes,[12] more men will observe their religious duties, and you will free yourselves from this man's pollution.

2.4

[1] Look! I willingly entrust myself to misfortune,[13] which they say I am wrong to blame, and to these enemies of mine: although I fear the enormity of their slander, I have confidence in your intelligence and in the truth of my actions. If they prevent me from even lamenting my present misfortune before you, I don't know where else to seek refuge. [2] Their slanderous accusations are pure invention—or should I call them evil intention? They pretend to be prosecuting and

---

[11] I.e., if the jurors fail to convict the killer, they themselves will, in effect, be the killers and will be polluted.

[12] That a conviction will deter others from committing crimes is a commonplace in prosecution speeches.

[13] Apparently an allusion to the fact that he could have gone into exile before delivering his second speech. This may suggest that Antiphon considers the defendant's case fairly strong; cf. 4.4.1n.

punishing a case of murder, but they reject all valid suspicion and call me the murderer simply because they don't know who really killed him. Their duty is to punish the killer, but their goal is evidently just the opposite, to kill me unjustly. [3] My proper course is only to defend myself against the attendant's testimony, for I am not obliged to reveal or convict the true killers, only to answer the charge against me. Nonetheless, I must do more if I am to make it entirely clear to you that these men are plotting against me and that I am free of all suspicion. [4] So I ask that my misfortune, which they use to criticize me, be turned to good fortune and that you delight me with an acquittal rather than pity me after a conviction.

They assert that anyone who happened on them during the attack would be more likely to investigate exactly who the killers were and report them when they reached home than to run away. [5] But I don't think any man is so brave or reckless that if in the middle of the night he came upon corpses still quivering, he wouldn't turn and run away rather than risk his life trying to learn the identity of the criminals. And since they surely preferred to do what was reasonable, it would be unreasonable to let those who killed them for their cloaks go free. Thus I am no longer a suspect. [6] Whether or not any other crimes were reported at the same time as the murder, who knows? No one took the trouble to look into this. So, since nothing is known of any such report, it is not implausible that he was killed by these criminals. [7] And why should you believe the attendant's testimony rather than that of free men?[14] If it is determined that the latter have testified falsely, they lose their civic rights and are fined, but this man furnished no proof and was not tortured, so how will he be punished?[15] Indeed, what proof could there be? Since he faced no danger in testifying, it's not surprising he was persuaded by his owners, my enemies, to lie about me. But it would be a sacrilege if this untrustworthy testimony

---

[14]There is, of course, no testimony from free men in this case, but the argument is valid that without any threat of punishment, the slave could say just what his masters wished. A free witness could face a suit for false witness (*pseudomartyria*); three convictions on this charge resulted in the loss of civic rights.

[15]In this case, the slave is already dead, and so the question of his punishment is moot. But Antiphon includes the generic argument that slaves have no reason to provide true testimony except under torture in order to demonstrate its use.

should cause you to destroy me. [8] They also assert that it is more plausible that I was present at the scene of the murder than absent, but I shall prove my absence not as a matter of likelihood but as a fact. I offer you all my slaves for torture, male and female;[16] if it becomes clear that I was not at home in bed that night or that I went out anywhere, then I admit I am the murderer. It was no ordinary night, for the man died the day of the Dipolieia.[17] [9] As for their claim that it is likely that I killed him because I was afraid of losing my prosperity, the situation is just the opposite. It is those in misfortune who stand to gain by stirring up trouble,[18] since in a time of change their own impoverished state can be expected to change. Those who are prosperous, on the other hand, stand to gain from preserving stability and protecting their present prosperity, for when conditions change, their fortune becomes misfortune. [10] Although they claim to establish my guilt on the basis of likelihood, they then assert that I am the man's killer not in likelihood but in fact. But it has been shown that the likelihood is on my side; moreover, the witness' testimony against me has been proven to be unconvincing, and it cannot be tested. Thus, I have shown that the evidence supports me not him and that the tracks of the murder lead not to me but to those who are being set free by my opponents.

Since their entire case has proven unconvincing, my acquittal would not mean that criminals cannot be proved guilty, but my con-

---

[16] According to the rules, challenges to torture a slave (1.6n) had to be issued before the trial, though occasionally one is issued during a trial (Aes. 2.126–128). Antiphon's purpose in not mentioning this alibi until nearly the end of the Tetralogy may be to illustrate that facts (*erga*) produce a more powerful argument than likelihood (*eikos*); it was the absence of facts, of course, that necessitated the *eikos* arguments in the first place. Note that the alibi, if accepted, only proves that he was not at the scene of the murder; he could still have been the "planner" (cf. 2.3.5) and enlisted an agent to commit the crime.

[17] An annual festival in honor of Zeus Polieus in the month Skirophorion (roughly June); see H. W. Parke, *Festivals of the Athenians* (London 1977): 162–167. The inclusion of such details would help confirm an alibi.

[18] The verb *neoterizein* means "innovate," often with the implication "make revolution." The general point that the rich do not foment change is irrelevant to the prosecution's argument about motive, but the implication that the rich do not engage in this sort of street crime may carry some weight.

viction would mean that no one facing prosecution can present a successful defense. [11] Their prosecution is unjust; they claim to be pure while seeking to murder me in unholy fashion and then calling my actions unholy though I only urge you to respect the gods. Since I am innocent of all charges, for myself I implore you to respect the righteousness of those who have done no wrong; I remind you that the dead man needs retribution, and I urge you not to convict an innocent man while you let the guilty go free. For if I am put to death, no longer will anyone search for the actual killer. [12] With these considerations in mind, acquit me in accordance with the laws of gods and men. Do not wait until later to change your mind and recognize your mistake, for later regret is no cure for such mistakes.

3. SECOND TETRALOGY

~~~~~~

Some young men were practicing javelin-throwing, when a boy who ran out on the field to pick up the javelins was accidentally struck and killed. The young man who threw the javelin is now charged with unintentional homicide (which would be tried in Athens at the Palladium by the Ephetae); the penalty is exile for a limited period, perhaps a year. Plutarch (*Pericles* 36.3) reports that after a competitor was killed in a similar situation, Pericles and Protagoras spent an entire day discussing whether the javelin or the thrower or the organizers of the contest were responsible for his death "according to the most correct argument" (*logos*). Whether or not an actual incident gave rise to these discussions, the story indicates that the issue of cause and responsibility with regard to accidents occupied the attention of intellectuals at this time.

In contrast to the First Tetralogy, the facts of this case are not in dispute; because of this, the plaintiff at first assumes there is no question about the verdict, but the defendant presents what he himself admits is a very subtle argument (3.2.2), that his son is not responsible for the boy's death since the boy is responsible for his own death. Antiphon seems to be indicating that the plaintiff presents the normal or traditional view of this sort of case, whereas the defendant's arguments represent new, sophisticated reasoning that may be viewed with suspicion by many.

The defendant's argument rests on a complex assessment of each person's behavior by comparison with the behavior of others in the same situation: the young man did the same thing as the other young men who were throwing javelins, but the boy behaved differently from the other bystanders, who did not run out on the field. By setting the issue in terms of mistake (*hamartia*) and by comparing the two parties' actions to those of others at the scene, Antiphon comes close to a modern concept of negligence in terms of a "reasonable man" standard of behavior. We could also see the issue as the legal and moral responsibility for an act of which a person is (to use modern terms) a necessary but not a sufficient cause (cf. Arist., *Nicomachaean Ethics* 3.1–5). Athenian law almost certainly did not lay down precise guidelines for such situations, and it is unclear what conclusions jurors would reach if this were a real case.

3.1

[1] When the facts are agreed on by both sides, the verdict is determined by the laws and by those who voted,[1] who have final authority over our government; but if there is disagreement on any matter, it is your duty, citizens, to decide. In this case I think even the defendant will not disagree with me; for my boy,[2] struck in the side on the training field by a javelin thrown by this young man, died on the spot. I therefore charge him not with intentional but with unintentional homicide. [2] For me, of course, the misfortune he unintentionally caused is just as great as if he had acted intentionally; he has not burdened the spirit of the dead man but of those still living. So I beg you, pity the parents' loss of their child, mourn for the deceased's unseasonable death, ban the killer from the places prescribed in the law,[3] and do not ignore the pollution he has brought on the whole city.

3.2

[1] It is now clear that misfortune and need force even those who mind their own business[4] to appear in court, to grow bold though

---

[1] This seems to mean "those who voted in the Assembly to approve the laws"; but the expression is unclear and the text may be damaged.

[2] "Boy" and "young man" are used consistently to distinguish the two; the latter is perhaps 16 or 17 years old, the former several years younger.

[3] Athenian law specified several public and religious places, including the Agora, where the lawcourts were, as off limits to those formally accused or convicted of homicide.

[4] The *topos* (cf. above, 1.1n) of "minding one's own business" (*apragmōn*) is commonly contrasted with the "busybody" (*polypragmōn*), who is excessively fond of litigation.

they are normally quiet, and in general to speak and act against their nature. Unless I am greatly mistaken, I am not and have no desire to be such a person, but I am now forced by this very misfortune to behave in an unaccustomed manner in defending myself.[5] This is a case whose precise meaning I can hardly understand, and I am even more perplexed how I should explain it to you. [2] So I am forced by cruel necessity to seek refuge, jurors, in your pity. I beg you, if you think I speak with greater than usual subtlety,[6] do not, because of circumstances just mentioned, judge my defense by appearance (*doxa*) rather than truth (*alētheia*). For the appearance of things favors those who speak well, but the truth favors those who act in a just and righteous manner.

[3] I thought it would be good for both of us if I taught my son things that brought the greatest benefit to the community, but the result has been very different from what I expected. For the young man, not through any insolence (*hybris*) or lack of self-control (*akolasia*)[7] but simply practicing with his friends on the playing field, threw his javelin but did not kill anyone, according to the truth of what he did;[8] however, he is now unwillingly blamed for someone else's accidental self-injury. [4] Now, if the javelin had hit and wounded the boy because it carried outside the boundaries of its proper course, then we would have no argument (*logos*) against the charge of homicide. But because the boy ran under the trajectory of the javelin and placed his body in its path, one of them was prevented from hitting the target, whereas the other was hit because he ran under the javelin. And now

---

[5] The defense (3.2 and 3.4) is presented by the father of the defendant, who is apparently not old enough to defend himself. The father often speaks as if he himself is on trial. In a sense he is, since if he loses, he might have to accompany his son into exile, but his pleas do not (and are not intended to) present a clear or consistent picture of the potential punishment.

[6] *Akribeia* ("precision, subtlety") was a common term characterizing the new intellectual ideas of the sophists.

[7] Cf. 4.1.6.

[8] "According to the truth of what he did" is a literal translation. The Greek suggests that the young man's actions can be understood in different ways: their appearance is that the young man killed the boy, but their truth is that he did not. Cf. 3.3.3, 3.4.2.

he hits us with the blame, though it is in no way ours! [5] Since the boy was hit because of his running under, the young man is unjustly accused, for he hit none of those who were standing away from the target. If it is clear to you that the boy was not hit while standing still but while intentionally running under the trajectory of the javelin, then this shows even more clearly that he died on account of his own mistake (*hamartia*), for he would not have been hit if he had stood still and hadn't run.

[6] Since, as you know, both sides agree that the killing was unintentional, the killer can be determined even more clearly by establishing which of the two made the mistake. Those who because of a mistake fail to accomplish what they have in mind to do are the agents of unintentional acts, and those who do or experience anything unintentional are responsible for their sufferings.[9] [7] Now the young man made no mistake affecting anyone, for he was practicing what was assigned, not what was prohibited; he was throwing his javelin on the throwing field, not where others were exercising; and he did not hit the boy because he missed his target and threw toward the bystanders; rather, he did everything he intended to do correctly, did nothing unintentional, and suffered by being prevented from hitting his target. [8] The boy, on the other hand, wished to run out but mistook the right moment to run out without being hit and fell into unwanted misfortune. By his unintentional mistake against himself he experienced his own misfortune, but he has punished himself for his mistake and thus has his just deserts. It's not something we want or enjoy, for we share his pain and his suffering. Since the mistake is his, the act is not ours but results from his mistake; and since the suffering afflicts the doer, we are relieved of blame, and the doer is punished at the very moment of his mistake. [9] We are also acquitted by the law on which he relies in prosecuting me for murder, the law that prohibits killing unjustly or justly.[10] Because of the dead boy's own mistake, the young

---

[9] The text of this sentence is in doubt.

[10] "Unjustly or justly" here apparently mean "intentionally or unintentionally," as the following sentence makes clear. On the surface this "law" seems contradictory (how can a law prohibit "just killing"?), but if we understand it (as the litigants clearly do) to prohibit intentional and unintentional killing, then it becomes a summary statement of Athenian homicide law.

man is acquitted of killing him unintentionally, and because the plaintiff does not even accuse him of intentional killing, he is acquitted on both counts, intentional and unintentional killing.

[10] Since we are thus acquitted by the truth of what was done and by the law under which they prosecute, it is not right that just because of our ordinary activities we should be thought to deserve such troubles. This young man will suffer unholy evils if he has to pay for mistakes that are not his, while I, who am just as innocent as he is but not more, will encounter much greater misfortune. If he is ruined, the rest of my life will be unlivable, and my childlessness will be a tomb while I still live. [11] So, take pity on this young man, whose misfortune is not his fault, and on me, this wretched old man, whose suffering was so unexpected. Do not vote for conviction and consign us to a miserable fate, but respect the gods and acquit us. The victim is not unavenged for the misfortune he fell into,[11] and it is not right for us to bear a share of his errors. [12] So have respect for the righteousness and justice of these actions, acquit us as is right and just, and do not cast the two of us, father and son, a most wretched pair, into an untimely disaster.

3.3

[1] I think this man has shown by actions (*erga*), not words (*logoi*),[12] that need can compel anyone to speak and act against his nature. In the past he wasn't the least bit disrespectful or daring, but now he is compelled by misfortune itself to make statements I never imagined he would utter. [2] In my foolishness I didn't think he would even give a response; otherwise I would not have given just one speech instead of two and deprived myself of half of my prosecution.[13] And if

---

[11] This point is explained further below, 3.4.8–10.

[12] The complex relationship of *ergon* ("act, deed, reality") and *logos* ("speech, argument, reason") interested many Greeks at this time, most notably Thucydides, who employs speeches in part to give meaning to the events he narrates. Here the pairing does little but foreshadow later, more significant instances (3.3.3, 3.4.2).

[13] I.e., his first speech presented essentially no arguments, since he assumed none would be needed, and so he now has only one speech for all his arguments. However, the plaintiff's second speech is substantially longer than either of the defendant's speeches.

he were not so daring, he would not have this double advantage of giving one speech in defense against my one speech and have his one speech of accusation go unanswered.[14] [3] With such an advantage over us in his words and a much greater advantage in his actions, he makes this outrageous request that you accept his defense completely. By contrast, I have done nothing wrong but have suffered terrible miseries and now suffer even more terribly. So, gentlemen—you who punish evil deeds and distinguish righteous actions—I seek refuge in your pity in fact, not in word, and I make this request: where the facts are clear, don't let yourselves be persuaded by a wicked subtlety of words to think that the truth of what was done is really false.[15] [4] For subtlety is persuasive rather than true, while truth is less deceitful but also less powerful. If I put my trust in justice, I can ignore the defendant's arguments, but I distrust the cruel hand of divinity and dread the possibility not only of losing the benefit of my son but also of seeing him condemned by you as a murderer.

[5] He has the audacity and the insolence to claim that his son, who both threw and killed, did not wound or kill; and he asserts that my son, who did not touch the javelin and never even thought of throwing it, missed the whole earth and everyone else on it and thrust the javelin through his own ribs. I think I could make a more convincing case for intentional homicide than this man can when he asserts that the young man neither threw nor killed. [6] For the boy was summoned at the right moment by the trainer,[16] who was in charge of picking up the javelins for the throwers, but because of the thrower's lack of self-control, he encountered this young man's hostile missile and died miserably, though he had made no mistake affecting anyone. But the young man made a mistake about the right moment for picking up the javelins. He wasn't prevented from hitting his target; no, he hit a most wretched and bitter target. He didn't kill intentionally, but it would be more accurate to say he killed intentionally than to say he did not throw or kill at all. [7] Although he killed my boy un-

---

[14] I.e., the defendant's first speech was, in effect, a prosecution speech accusing the boy of killing himself.

[15] Cf. above, 3.2.2n, 3.2.3n, and 3.3.1n.

[16] In a real case the role of this trainer might receive more attention, but Antiphon does not wish to pursue this issue here (cf. 3.4.4).

intentionally no less than if he had intended to, he denies killing him at all and claims he is not convicted even by the law prohibiting just and unjust homicide. But who threw the javelin? Who is to be credited with the killing? The spectators or the attendants, whom no one accuses of anything? There is nothing obscure about his death; for me it is all too clear. I say the law is correct to prescribe punishment for those who kill, since it's right that someone who kills when he did not intend to kill have troubles he did not intend to have, but it would be wrong for the victim to be left unavenged, since he suffers just as much from unintentional as from intentional harm. [8] And it's wrong to acquit him just because his mistake was unfortunate. If misfortune is not caused by divine involvement, then it's right for the person who erred to suffer the consequences of his mistake; but if a divine pollution falls on the agent for some impious act, it would not be right to prevent divine retribution.

[9] They also argue that because of their exemplary life, they shouldn't be thought to deserve such troubles. But how could we deserve our suffering, when we have led just as good a life and are punished with death? When he claims he made no mistake and argues that those who make mistakes deserve misfortune but not those who make no mistake, he is arguing our case. For my son made no mistake affecting anyone but was killed by this young man; it would be wrong if he is not avenged. And I too will suffer dreadfully, though I'm even less guilty of error than he, if you don't give me the revenge granted by the law. [10] I shall now demonstrate on the basis of their own statements that he cannot be absolved of the mistake or the unintentional homicide but that both of these belong to the boy and the young man together. If it's right to consider the boy his own killer because he ran into the path of the javelin and didn't stand still, then the young man is not free from blame either, but only if he was standing still and not throwing his javelin when the boy died. But since both contributed to the killing, and the boy has already punished himself more severely than warranted by a mistake that affected only himself—for he's dead—then surely it's not right that his accomplice and partner in a mistake affecting those who didn't deserve it at all should escape without penalty.

[11] Thus, on the basis of their own defense speech, the young man shares responsibility for the killing, and it would be unjust and un-

godly for you to acquit him. We have already been destroyed by their mistake; if you now convict us of murder, you would make us suffer not righteously but unrighteously. And if those who have brought us this death are not banned from the appropriate places,[17] your acquittal of those who are unholy would be disrespectful of the gods.[18] Since the entire pollution of everyone will come on you, you must exercise great caution. If you convict him and ban him from the places restricted by law, you will remain innocent of the charges, but if you acquit him, you are guilty. [12] So, for the sake of your righteousness and the laws, take him off and punish him. Don't share in this person's pollution yourselves; and for us the parents, already living in this tomb because of him, make this disaster at least seem lighter.

3.4

[1] My opponent was probably thinking about his own prosecution speech and didn't understand my defense, but your task is to recognize that we litigants judge a matter from our own point of view, and we each naturally assume our own case is just.[19] You, however, must examine the facts impartially, [2] for the truth of these facts is only discernible from what each side says.[20] For my part, if I have lied about anything, I agree that whatever I have said correctly can also be discredited as unfair; but if I have spoken the truth but with subtlety and precision, then it is only fair that any hostility that results should be directed not at me the speaker but at him (the boy) who acted.

[3] First, I want you to understand that a man is not a killer if someone claims he is but only if he is proven to be. The defendant here agrees that the actions occurred as we have stated, but he disagrees on the question of the killer, although it is impossible to show who the killer is in any other way than from the actions. [4] He complains that his son is being slandered if he is shown to be a killer when he did not throw a javelin or even think of throwing one, but he is

---

[17] See 3.1.2n.

[18] There is uncertainty about the text here.

[19] This is an extraordinarily frank statement of a litigant's natural bias; such a sentiment would probably not be expressed by a real litigant.

[20] For the relation between facts and words, see 3.3.1n.

not addressing my argument. I'm not saying the boy threw a javelin or hit himself with it but that by going under the javelin's blow he was killed not by the young man but by himself; for he did not die standing still. And since this running is to blame, then if he ran out because he was called by the trainer, the trainer would be the one who killed him, but if he ran out on his own impulse, then he was killed by himself. [5] I don't want to move to another point before making it even clearer whose act it was. The young man did not miss his target any more than any of his fellow practicers, nor did he do anything he is accused of through his own mistake; but the boy didn't act in the same way as his fellow spectators but ran out into the path of the javelin. This shows clearly that because of his own error he met with greater misfortunes than those who stood still. The thrower would not have missed his target if no one had run under his javelin; and the boy would not have been hit if he had stayed with the spectators. [6] I shall now demonstrate that the young man has no greater share in the killing than his fellow throwers. If the boy died because the young man threw his javelin, then all his fellow practicers would share responsibility for the act, since the reason they didn't hit him is not because they didn't throw their javelins but because he did not run under any of their javelins. The young man did not make a mistake any more than they did; just like them he would not have hit the boy if he had stood still with the other spectators. [7] The boy not only made a mistake, he also was careless. The young man saw no one running across the field, so how could he have taken care not to hit anyone? But the boy saw the javelin-throwers and could easily have taken care that no one hit him, for he could have stood still. [8] As for the law they cite, we should praise it, for it correctly and justly punishes those who kill unintentionally with unintended sufferings. Since the young man made no mistake, it would not be fair for him to be punished for someone else's mistake; it is enough for him to bear the consequences of his own mistakes. But the boy was destroyed by his own mistake, and the moment he erred, he also punished himself. Therefore, the killer is punished and the death is not unavenged.

[9] Since the killer has already been punished, you will not leave an avenging spirit if you acquit us but only if you convict us. Since the boy himself bears the consequences of his own mistake, he will not leave behind an avenging spirit; but the young man is innocent of all

blame, and so if he is destroyed, his spirit will be a greater burden on those who convict him.[21] If by our speeches the boy is revealed to be a killer, the blame for this falls not on us, the speakers, but on the deeds that were done. [10] Since these proofs have correctly proven that the boy is the killer, the law absolves us of any blame and convicts the actual killer. So, don't cast us into troubles we don't deserve, and don't lend assistance to them in their misfortunes by rendering a verdict contrary to the divinity. Rather, in accordance with divine and human justice, remember that this unfortunate event occurred because of his running under the path of the javelin, and acquit us. We are not to blame for the killing.

---

[21] There is considerable exaggeration here, since the penalty for a conviction is exile, not death.

4. THIRD TETRALOGY

This is the shortest of the Tetralogies and lacks the concentrated focus found in the first two. The case concerns a death resulting from a fight when both men had apparently been drinking, circumstances that were probably as common in Athens as they are today. As in the Second Tetralogy, questions are raised about the two men's intentions and the victim's own responsibility for his death. A third possible agent is also introduced, the doctor who attended the victim before his death, though under Athenian law a doctor could not normally be held responsible for the death of his patient. Although some cases of killing in self-defense, such as killing an attacker on the highway, could be categorized as "lawful homicide" and tried at the Delphinium (see Dem. 23.53 and *Ath. Pol.* 57.3), this case is probably envisaged as being tried as intentional homicide at the Areopagus. If the victim started the fight (and the plaintiff in this case never explicitly denies this), this could bolster the defense against a charge of intentional homicide but did not automatically make the killing lawful.[1] A similar case is mentioned in Demosthenes 21.73–75.

The defendant certainly seems to have the weaker case, and Antiphon probably intends to underline this weakness by having him leave for exile before his second speech, which is delivered by friends. Although the jurors still could decide for the defendant, his departure undoubtedly conveyed the strong impression of lack of confidence and thus probably made a conviction more likely.

---

[1] Contrast the treatment of a case involving the killing of an adulterer caught in the act (Lys. 1).

4.1

[1] It is a well-established rule that prosecutors in homicide cases should make every effort to make their case and present their witnesses in accordance with justice and not let the guilty go free or bring the innocent to trial. [2] When god wished to make the human race, he brought forth the first of us humans and provided the earth and the sea as our sustenance so that we would not die from lack of basic necessities before reaching old age.² Since god placed such a high value on our life, whoever kills someone unlawfully sins against the gods and violates the rules of human society. [3] The victim, deprived of the gift god gave him, is likely to leave behind hostile avenging spirits as god's instrument of vengeance; and if unjust prosecutors and witnesses have shared in the killer's sin, they will take this pollution into their own homes, though it was not originally theirs. [4] Thus, if we the avengers of the dead prosecute the innocent for an ulterior motive, then we will not only be afflicted by the victim's vengeance, since we are not avenging his death, but we also face punishment for murder for unjustly killing an innocent man. Finally, we also assume responsibility for your error if we persuade you to do something unlawful. [5] Fearing all this, I have brought the true sinner to you and thus remain free from such charges. For your part, these considerations mean that you must give your verdict the full attention it deserves and assign the criminal a penalty appropriate to the suffering he has caused; in this way you will keep the entire city free of pollution.

[6] If he had killed the man unintentionally, he would deserve some leniency, but since he killed an old man in drunken arrogance (*hybris*) and without self-control (*akolasia*),³ hitting and choking him till he could no longer breathe, he is liable for punishment for murder. And

---

²There is no standard Greek myth of human creation, but the sophists took great interest in the creation and early history of humans. Protagoras recounts a myth of Prometheus and the creation of humans in Plato, *Protagoras* 320c–322d (cf. Aeschylus, *Prometheus* 439–506, Euripides, *Suppliants* 201–218), and Democritus may have devised an account of early human society. Antiphon here also alludes to a common sophistic theme in suggesting that *physis*, or (human) nature, provides a foundation for *nomos*, or law; see further Kerferd 1981: 111–130.

³Cf. 3.2.3.

since he violated all the rules about treating the elderly, he rightly deserves all the punishment appropriate for such criminals.

[7] The law is correct to deliver him to you for punishment. You have heard the witnesses who were with him when he was drunk. You must stem the lawlessness of this injury, punish his arrogance for the suffering he caused, and take away his life as he took away another's by this deed he planned.

4.2

[1] I'm not surprised they have kept their speech short, for they did not run the risk of suffering harm themselves but of ruining me unjustly in their hatred. But it's only natural I think that I'm upset at them for wanting to put this case on the level of the most serious crimes, since the victim was actually more responsible for his own death than I was. He began the fight by drunkenly attacking someone much more sober, and so he is responsible not just for his own misfortune but also for this charge against me.

[2] I don't think their accusation is either just or righteous. He hit me first, and even if I had defended myself with a sword or a rock or a stick, I still wouldn't be wrong, since those who start a fight should rightly be repaid not in the same degree but more severely. He hit me with his hands, and I returned the blows with my own hands. Was that wrong? [3] Well, he'll say that "the law prohibiting just and unjust killing shows that you are liable for the penalties for homicide; for the man is dead."[4] For the second and third time I say that I did not kill him. If the man had died from the blows on the spot, then his death would be attributable to me, though it would still be just, for justice requires that those who start a fight be repaid not in the same degree but more severely. [4] But as it was, he was entrusted to the care of a bad doctor and died many days later not from the blows but because of the doctor's incompetence.[5] Other doctors warned him that although he could be cured, he would die if he followed that course of treatment. But you his advisers caused his death, which has led to

---

[4] For this "law," see 3.2.9 and note.

[5] In Athens a doctor could not be prosecuted for homicide if a patient died after receiving treatment; see 4.3.5.

this unholy charge against me. [5] I am also acquitted by the law under which I am being prosecuted,[6] since it provides that the plotter of a death is a killer. But how could I have plotted to kill him unless he plotted to kill me too? I used the same means in defending myself against him; I did the same to him as he did to me, and clearly he plotted the same against me as I plotted against him. [6] If someone thinks he died from the blows and considers me the man's killer, he should conclude instead that because the blows were caused by the initiator of the fight, he clearly is responsible for the death and not I, since I would not have defended myself if I had not been struck by him. So, since I am acquitted by the law and by the fact that he started the fight, I am not in any way his killer. The victim is the killer, and if it was unfortunate that he died, he was the victim of his own misfortune, since he had the misfortune to start the fight. But if he died through thoughtlessness, then it was his own thoughtlessness, for he wasn't thinking well when he struck me.

[7] I have demonstrated that I am unjustly accused; I now wish to show that my accusers are themselves liable to all the charges they are bringing against me. By plotting to murder me, though I am innocent of all blame, and depriving me of the life god gave me, they sin against god; by plotting my death unjustly, they violate all human laws and become in fact my murderers; and by persuading you to put me to death in this unholy fashion, they also become murderers of your righteousness. [8] Let god punish them. You [jurors], however, must consider your own interest and be willing to acquit, not convict me. If I am wrongly acquitted and get off because you were incorrectly informed, then I will set the dead man's spirit of vengeance on the person who did not inform you, not on you; but if I am wrongly convicted by you, I will inflict the wrath of his avenging spirits on you, not on him. [9] Understand then that the offense against god is theirs

---

[6] The speaker refers to Athenian homicide law, which provides that the "planner" or instigator of a homicide was liable to the same treatment as the actual killer (And. 1.94). "Plotting" (*epibouleusas*) is a stronger form of "planning" (*bouleusas*); see further Introduction to Antiphon 6. Although the defendant in this case is accused of killing the victim himself, not by planning, the prosecutor's allusion to planning (4.1.7) provides an opening for this line of defense.

and that you yourselves are blameless, and acquit me as is just and righteous. In this way all our citizens would remain completely pure.

4.3

[1] It doesn't surprise me that this man's words match the unholy acts he has committed, and I understand that in your desire to learn precisely what happened you would put up with hearing arguments from him that deserve to be rejected out of hand. He agrees he struck the blows that led to the death, but he says he's not the victim's murderer; instead, though he lives and breathes, he accuses us of being his murderer, though we seek only revenge. I want to show that the rest of his defense has arguments similar to these.

[2] His first argument is that although the man died from his blows, he didn't kill him, because by law the initiator of the fight is to blame for what happened and should be convicted, and the victim started the fight. But first of all, you know that young men are more likely (*eikos*) to get drunk and start a fight than old men; for they are proud of their birth, at their peak physically, and not used to drinking, all of which arouses them to anger. Old men, however, tend to control themselves, since they are used to drinking, are weak in old age, and fear the strength of the young. [3] The deed itself indicates that he did not use the same means to defend himself but just the opposite, for he killed the man with hands then at their peak of strength, whereas the victim could not defend himself against the stronger man and died leaving no sign of any defense. And if he killed with his hands and not with a sword, he is all the more the killer, since his hands are more part of him than a sword. [4] Then he has the audacity to say that one who started the fight but didn't kill is the murderer rather than the person who killed, since (he says) he was the one who planned the death. But I say the opposite. If our hands are servants of our intentions, then the one who hit but didn't kill only planned the blow, but the one who struck the fatal blow planned the death; for the man is dead as a result of his intentional act. The one who struck the blow has met with misfortune; the one who was hit has met with disaster. The victim died because of that man's act, not through his own mistake but the defendant's; for in striking the blow he did more than he wished, and through his own misfortune he killed a man he didn't

wish to. [5] I'm surprised that in claiming the man died in the doctor's hands he also says we killed him by advising him to see the doctor; but if we had not advised him, he would say the man had died from our neglect. And even if he did die in the doctor's hands (which he didn't), the doctor is not his killer, for the law protects him.[7] We sent him to the doctor only because of this man's blows, so how could anyone else be his killer but the man who forced us to employ the doctor?

[6] We have clearly proven by every argument that he killed the man, but he has the audacity and the insolence not only to defend his ungodly actions but to accuse us of outrageous and unholy acts when we are bringing a prosecution against this man's pollution. [7] Of course, considering what he's done, it's fitting that he should say these things and even worse. For our part, we have demonstrated clearly how he died, there is agreement about the blow that caused his death, and the law assigns the murder to the one who struck the blow. So, we implore you to act on behalf of the dead man and appease the wrath of the avenging spirits with this man's death, thus making the city free of his pollution.

4.4

[1] The defendant has left[8] not because he recognizes his own guilt but because he fears the prosecutor's aggressiveness. As his friends, we think it more righteous to defend him while still alive than when he's dead. It would be best, of course, if he could give his own defense, but he thought it would be safer, so it is left to us to defend him, since we would be most grieved by losing him.

[2] In my opinion, to decide about the injustice we must determine who started the fight. The prosecutor uses improbable arguments in claiming this man started it. If it were a law of nature that just as we see with our eyes and hear with our ears, so too the young are aggressive and the old act with restraint, then we would not need

---

[7] See 4.2.4n.

[8] If the defendant voluntarily went into exile before his second speech, relatives or friends would give his final speech, and the jurors would still deliver their verdict. Antiphon may mean the defendant's departure here to suggest the weakness of his case.

your judgment, for age alone would convict young men. But many young men act with restraint, and many of the elderly become violent when drunk, so this argument does not support the prosecutor any more than the defendant. [3] Since this argument supports both sides equally, the entire advantage is ours, since the witnesses say the deceased started the fight; and since he started it, the defendant is blameless on all the other charges against him. For if the striker, by striking a blow and forcing you to seek the care of a doctor, is the murderer rather than the one who killed him,[9] then the initiator of the fight is in fact the murderer; for he compelled the other to strike back in self-defense and the one who was then struck to go to the doctor. It would be an awful experience for the defendant if he is declared the murderer instead of the actual killer, though he did not kill, and the initiator of the fight instead of the actual initiator, though he did not start it. [4] The defendant did not plot the death any more than the plaintiff. For if the initiator of the fight had intended to strike but not kill and the defender had intended to kill, then the latter would be the plotter, but he too intended to strike, not kill; he just made a mistake, and his blow had unintended results. [5] He planned the blow, but how could he have plotted the death, if his blow had unintended results? And the mistake belongs in fact to the initiator rather than the one who hit back, who was only seeking to return the blow he suffered when he was forced into a mistake by his assailant. But everything this one did or suffered resulted from his own lack of self-control; so he is responsible for his own and the other man's mistake and can justly be declared the murderer. [6] I shall now demonstrate that the blows he struck in self-defense were not stronger but much weaker than those he suffered. The other man acted entirely out of drunken arrogance, with no thought of self-defense, but the defendant only wanted to avoid suffering and ward off the blows; what he suffered was involuntary, and in trying to avoid suffering he did less than the initiator of the fight deserved. It was self-defense, not aggression. [7] Even if his

---

[9] I.e., the doctor. The argument envisages a chain of causation: if we move responsibility from the immediate cause of death (the doctor) to an earlier cause (the striker), then we should also move it back to an even earlier cause (the starter of the fight).

own greater strength made his blows stronger than those he suffered, it isn't right to convict him; for large penalties are everywhere prescribed for the initiator of a fight, but nowhere is any penalty written for someone who defends himself. [8] The argument about the prohibition of just and unjust homicide has already been answered: the man did not die from the blows but from the doctor's care, as the witnesses have testified. The misfortune thus belongs to the initiator of the fight, not the defender. The latter acted and suffered unintentionally and became involved in someone else's misfortune, but the initiator did everything intentionally: he brought this fortune on himself by his own actions, and by his own misfortune he erred. [9] It has now been shown that the defendant is not liable on any of the charges. But if someone thinks the deed and the misfortune belong to both parties jointly and decides on the basis of the arguments presented that the defendant is equally deserving of acquittal and conviction, even in that case it's right to acquit rather than convict him. For it's unjust for someone to gain a conviction without showing clearly that he has been wronged, and it's wrong to convict a defendant unless the charge has been clearly proven.

[10] The defendant has now been completely cleared of the charges, and so our plea on his behalf is even more righteous: in your desire to punish the killer do not put an innocent man to death. If you do, the dead man's spirit will still be just as much an avenging spirit for those guilty of the crime, and the unholy destruction of this man will double the pollution brought by those spirits against those who killed him.[10] [11] Fearing this pollution, consider it your duty to free the innocent man from blame. As for the polluted killer, leave him to be revealed by time and punished by the victim's relatives. In this way you would do what is best for men and gods.

---

[10] I.e., in addition to the spirit of the original victim, the defendant, if unjustly convicted, will also haunt those guilty of unjustly killing him, namely, the plaintiff and the jurors. The speaker disregards the fact that the defendant is already in exile and thus would not be put to death or leave avenging spirits (cf. 3.4.9n). Moreover, the person guilty of the original homicide according to the defense, namely, the victim himself, has already been punished in full.

5. ON THE MURDER OF HERODES

Antiphon's longest surviving speech, *On the Murder of Herodes*, was regarded in antiquity as one of his best. Modern opinion generally agrees, though our ignorance on several important issues makes any assessment of the argument difficult. Being a defense speech, it can be selective in its narration of events, for the jurors would already have been given an account by the prosecution. The mixture of substantive and procedural issues also complicates our assessment.

The speech was delivered about a decade after the Mytilenean revolt in 427 BC. As reported by Thucydides (3.1–50), Mytilene, the main city on the island of Lesbos and one of Athens' most powerful and important allies in the Peloponnesian War, rebelled against Athenian dominance. Athens put down the revolt, executed its leaders, and sent Athenian settlers, who divided up the territory. The Mytileneans continued to farm the land, paying an annual rent. It is a reasonable guess that Herodes was one of these Athenian settlers. The speaker is a young Mytilenean, whose name, according to a late source, is Euxitheus. His father had played some part in this revolt (5.74–80) and was apparently living in voluntary exile in Thrace. We may imagine that the Athenian jurors would still have strong memories of the event and might be biased against any Mytilenean, though it is impossible to know how this would have affected their verdict.

The events, as best we can reconstruct them, are as follows: Euxitheus was traveling on the same boat as Herodes from Mytilene to Thrace, when they were forced by a storm to put in at a small harbor on the north shore of Lesbos. There they waited out the storm, drinking on another boat in the harbor, one that had a roof. Sometime during the night Herodes disappeared and was not seen again. A search was made, but no body was ever found. Euxitheus then continued to Thrace, but when he later returned to Mytilene, he was accused of murdering Herodes. In his absence Herodes' relatives had apparently interrogated a slave who initially denied any knowledge of the crime but later, under torture, confessed to assisting Euxitheus in the murder. His story was that they had killed Herodes on shore, striking him with a rock, and had dumped his body at sea from a small boat. The prosecution also presented an incriminating note, allegedly written by Euxitheus to a certain Lycinus. Both men had previously had dealings with Herodes. It is not clear what specific motive, if any, the prosecution gave for the crime. Euxitheus was then brought to Athens for trial.

In his defense, Euxitheus first argues vehemently against the procedure used to prosecute him (see below). He then disputes the facts, claiming the events that night happened by chance and could not have been planned and pointing to several contradictions in the prosecution's case. Euxitheus also emphasizes that the slave's story was extracted from him by torture when Euxitheus was absent, and the prosecution then put the slave to death, their purpose being (he says) to prevent Euxitheus from questioning him and exposing the truth. Another witness, a free man, had given different testimony, stating that Euxitheus never left the boat that night. Euxitheus also accuses the prosecution of planting the note to Lycinus and claims, moreover, that neither he nor Lycinus had any motive for killing Herodes. He concludes that the prosecution do not know who killed Herodes, and he accuses them rather vaguely of manufacturing the case against him for their own profit.

The procedural issue is thorny. The regular procedure for prosecuting a homicide case was a *dikē phonou* ("suit for homicide"), which would be tried before the Areopagus and supervised by the Basileus. Once the Basileus accepted the case, the accused was banned from most sacred and public places until the trial (3.1.2n) but was not otherwise constrained. Other special rules applied to homicide cases concerning such matters as oaths, and the accused could voluntarily go into exile any time before his second speech (4.4.1n). Euxitheus apparently came to Athens expecting to face a *dikē phonou*, but instead he was arrested by the special procedure of *apagōgē* (see Series Introduction) normally used against specific classes of common criminals called *kakourgoi* ("evil-doers"; see 2.1.4n). It could also be used against a killer caught in a place from which he was banned, but according to Euxitheus, it had never before been used for an ordinary case of homicide. Apparently the prosecution argued that this was legitimate, since homicide was a great evil deed (*kakourgēma*, 5.10), and the officials in charge of *apagōgē*, the Eleven, accepted the case.[1] The prosecution did not allow Euxitheus to post sureties, as was normally done, and so he was imprisoned until the trial. He is being tried in one of the popular courts (where most trials took place) before a large jury of ordinary citizens, rather than before the Areopagus. The reason for this irregular procedure may have been to ensure that he did not leave Athens before the trial. Since his father was living in Thrace, voluntary exile from Athens (and probably from Mytilene too) would probably not be much of a hardship for him. But the prosecution may have had other motives as well.

The prologue (1–7) is followed by arguments about the proper procedure for prosecution (8–19). Then comes the narrative, which includes some argument (20–24), arguments from likelihood (*eikos*, 25–28), the interrogation and testimony of the prosecution's witnesses (29–42), more arguments from likelihood (43–45), further discussion of the interrogation of the witnesses (46–52), and briefer discussions of the note to Lycinus (53–56), alleged motives (57–63), the need for certain proof (64–73), Euxitheus' father and the Mytilenean revolt (74–80), and signs from heaven (81–84). The epilogue (85–96) is devoted largely to the procedural issue discussed in 8–19. The verdict is unknown.

For further discussion of the issues in this case, see the notes to Edwards' translation in M. Edwards and S. Usher, eds., *Greek Orators*,

---

[1] The Eleven were the officials who supervised prisons, executions, and certain other matters, such as the *apagōgē* procedure. It is not clear how much authority they had. The Basileus in Antiphon 6 initially rejected a homicide case on technical grounds, and in Lysias 13 the Eleven forced the prosecutor to modify the wording of his indictment.

I, *Antiphon and Lysias* (Warminster, 1985) and M. Gagarin, *The Murder of Herodes* (Frankfurt am Main, 1989).

5

[1] I wish I had the ability to speak and the experience in practical matters equal to my recent troubles and misfortunes,[2] but my experience of the latter goes beyond what is proper, while my deficiency in the former leaves me at a disadvantage. [2] For when I had to endure physical suffering because of an improper accusation,[3] my experience was no help, and here, when my salvation lies in stating the facts truthfully, my inability to speak hurts me. [3] Before now many who lacked speaking ability were unconvincing in telling the truth and were destroyed for this very reason, that they were unable to make the truth clear; but many others who had speaking ability were convincing with their lies and were saved precisely because they lied. Thus, someone with little experience in legal contests is forced to address himself to the prosecution's words rather than the actual events and the truth of what happened.[4] [4] So, gentlemen, I will not make the usual request that you pay attention, which is what most litigants ask who have no confidence in themselves and assume you will be unjust—for it's a reasonable expectation among good men that even without requesting it the defendant will have your full attention, just as the prosecution did without requesting it. [5] So this is my request: if I make any mistakes in speaking, forgive me and realize that the error was caused by inexperience, not wickedness, but anything I say correctly is spoken with truth rather than cleverness. It is not right for someone who goes wrong in his actions to be saved by words or for one who has been correct in his actions to be ruined by words. A word is only a mistake

---

[2] For the *topos* of inexperience, cf. 1.1.

[3] Euxitheus refers to the use of the wrong procedure against him (see 5.8–19).

[4] For the dichotomy of words (*logoi*) and events (*erga*) in connection with "the truth of what happened," see 3.2.3n, 3.3.1n. In comparing the remarks on truth here (5.3–5) with those in the Second Tetralogy, however, one must remember that in a hypothetical exercise, Antiphon could make frank statements that would be inappropriate in a real case.

of the tongue, but a deed is a mistake of the mind. [6] A man who faces personal danger cannot avoid making some mistake, since he must consider not only his speech but his whole future; everything that is now unclear is more in the hands of fortune than foresight, and this will necessarily unnerve someone already in danger. [7] I have observed that even those with much experience in court do not speak as well as usual when they face danger, but when there is no danger, they are more successful. So, my request, gentlemen, is both legally and morally right—in accordance with your justice no less than my own. I shall now answer each of the charges in turn.

[8] First, I will demonstrate to you that I was brought to this trial by highly illegal and violent methods. It's not that I would avoid trial by you, the people:[5] even if you were not under oath or subject to any law, I would entrust my life to your verdict, since I am confident I have done no wrong in this matter and that your decision will be guided by justice. But I want you to treat this violent and illegal behavior as evidence of their treatment of me and their conduct in general. [9] My first point is that I was denounced[6] as a common criminal (*kakourgos*), though in fact I'm on trial for homicide,[7] something no one in this land has ever experienced before. The prosecution themselves bear witness that I am not a common criminal and am not subject to the law concerning them. That law concerns thieves and cloak-snatchers, and they have not shown that these are relevant to my case. So at least as regards this summary arrest (*apagōgē*), they have shown that both law and justice require my acquittal. [10] Then they say that homicide is surely a great crime. I agree, it's the greatest. But so are temple robbery and treason, and yet there are separate laws for each of these. In my case the prosecution have in the first place caused the trial to be held in the Agora,[8] the very place that is proclaimed off-limits for oth-

---

[5] I.e., by the popular court as opposed to the court of the Areopagus.

[6] The prosecution first issued an *endeixis* ("denunciation") requesting that the Eleven arrest Euxitheus by *apagōgē*. For *kakourgos*, see 2.1.4n.

[7] The Greek can also mean "I am being tried by a *dikē phonou*," which of course is not the case, though it should be.

[8] The popular courts were located in the Athenian Agora; the Areopagus met on a hill nearby. This case was probably tried in a roofed building called the Parabyston, where the Eleven presided; see Boegehold 1995: esp. 178–179.

ers on trial for homicide; and they have also made the case assessable,[9] when the law stipulates that the killer should be killed in turn. They did this not for my benefit but for their own profit, thereby giving the dead man less than the law provides. You will learn their reasons for this in the course of my speech.[10] [11] Second, as I think you all know, all courts judge homicide cases in the open air, for the simple reason that the jurors won't be together with someone with impure hands and so that the prosecutor of a homicide won't be under the same roof as the killer. You have evaded this law and done the opposite from others. Also, you ought to have sworn the greatest and strongest oath,[11] calling down destruction on yourself, your family, and your entire household and swearing to confine your case to this murder alone.[12] So, I would not be convicted for anything besides this act, even if I had committed many other crimes, and I would not be acquitted for my good deeds, no matter how many I had accomplished. [12] But you have evaded these rules: you invent laws for yourself, you prosecute me without swearing an oath, and your witnesses testify without swearing, though they ought to testify against me only after swearing the same oath as you with a hand on the sacrificial victims. And then you ask the jurors to convict me of homicide on the evidence of unsworn witnesses, though you have proven them untrustworthy by your own violations of the established laws. You must think your illegal conduct

---

[9] In some cases a penalty was not fixed by law but was decided after a guilty verdict by the jurors, who chose between penalties proposed by each side. The best-known example is the trial of Socrates, where after the guilty verdict the prosecutors proposed the death penalty, and Socrates countered by proposing a modest fine (see Plato's reconstruction in the *Apology*). The penalty in a *dikē phonou* was death, with exile as a practical alternative. The penalty in an *apagōgē* was normally death, but an assessment may sometimes have been made.

[10] This promise is apparently never fulfilled; it is not clear just how the prosecution would profit by this.

[11] The *diomosia* was a special oath sworn by litigants in a homicide case. Also in a homicide case, witnesses swore their support for the litigant's guilt or innocence, but in other cases witnesses were probably unsworn.

[12] There was no means to enforce the rule that one must stick to the subject in a homicide case; it was up to the jurors to decide whether such matters as previous service to the city were relevant.

should take precedence over the laws themselves! [13] You say that if I had been set free, I would not have awaited trial but would have departed, as if you had compelled me to come to this land unwillingly;[13] but if being banned from this city was of no concern to me, I could equally well have not come when summoned and lost the case by default, or I could have made my defense but left after my first speech.[14] This course is available to everyone, but you have enacted your own private law, trying to deprive me alone of something all other Greeks have. [14] I think everyone will agree that the laws governing these matters are the finest and most righteous of all laws. They are the oldest established laws in this land, and their main points have always remained the same,[15] which is the best sign of well-enacted laws; for time and experience teach people the faults in things. Therefore, you should not learn from the prosecutor's words whether the laws are good or not, but rather let the laws instruct you whether or not the prosecutor's words give an accurate account of the situation. [15] Thus the laws on homicide are the finest, and no one has ever dared change them. Only you have had the audacity to become a legislator and make them worse, seeking to ruin me unjustly in violation of these laws. Your violations are themselves the greatest evidence in my favor, for you are well aware that you would not have anyone testifying against me if they had had to swear the homicide oath. [16] Moreover, you did not have enough confidence in your case to set one conclusive trial on the matter, but you left room for further dispute and argument; evidently you lack confidence in these jurors as well. As a result, even an acquittal will do me no good, since you can say that I was acquitted of being a common criminal but not on the charge of homicide; on the other hand, if you win, you'll demand the death penalty on the ground that I was convicted of homicide. Could there be a more

---

[13] Euxitheus apparently expected to face a *dikē phonou*; he might not have been so willing to come to Athens, had he known what was planned for him.

[14] See 4.4.1n.

[15] After Draco enacted the first laws for Athens around 620 BC, Solon later (ca. 590) enacted new laws on everything except homicide, where Draco's laws continued in force. Draco's homicide law was still authoritative in the fifth century and was republished in 409/8; a damaged copy survives today. The sentiments in 5.14 are repeated in almost the same words in 6.2.

clever trap than this? If you persuade these men once, you'll have what you want, but if I am acquitted once, I'll still face the same danger! [17] There is more, gentlemen: my imprisonment was the most illegal act ever committed. I was willing to post three sureties,[16] as the law allows, but they would not let me do so. No other foreigner who was willing to post sureties has ever been imprisoned; and the officials in charge of cases of common criminals abide by this same law. So once more this law that applies to all other men fails to benefit me alone. [18] This was to their advantage, of course: first, I would be unprepared, since I could not attend to my own affairs, and second, I would suffer physically, and because of this my friends would become more willing to testify falsely on their side than to tell the truth on mine. They have also disgraced me and my family for the rest of our lives. [19] So, I have come to trial at a disadvantage with regard to your laws and justice. Even so, I'll try to demonstrate my innocence, though it is indeed hard to refute on the spot lies that have been carefully plotted for a long time now; one cannot take precautions against the unexpected.

[20] I made the journey from Mytilene in the same boat as Herodes, the man they say I killed. We were sailing to Aenus,[17] I to visit my father—for he happened to be there at the time—and Herodes to ransom prisoners to some Thracians. Also on the same boat were the prisoners who were to be ransomed and the Thracians who were going to pay the ransom. I present witnesses to these facts.

---

[16] A standard way of guaranteeing any promise, such as a debt, was to have friends (commonly three) stand surety; so Socrates' friends offer surety for his proposed fine in Plato's *Apology* (see above, 5.10n). We know of no other case where someone refuses to accept sureties, but the prosecutor's refusal, though unusual, was probably not illegal.

[17] Aenus was a Greek commercial city, paying tribute to Athens, near the mouth of the Hebrus river in Thrace. It was about 100 nautical miles from Mytilene; the journey would take about three days in normal conditions. From Mytilene one would sail north along the east coast of Lesbos and then west perhaps as far as Methymna, then directly north to Asia Minor, and then north along the coast to Aenus—never out of sight of land. It is likely that the boat left Mytilene early in the morning, encountered a storm in the early evening, and made it to shore before nightfall.

[WITNESSES]

[21] This was the reason we each had for the trip. We happened to encounter a storm, which forced us to put in to shore at a spot in the territory of Methymna.[18] Another boat was anchored there, and Herodes transferred to it before he died (as they say). But first consider this: these events took place by chance, not prearrangement, for no one has shown that I persuaded the man to sail with me. No, he made the journey on his own, for his own private business; [22] and I too clearly had sufficient reason of my own to make the journey to Aenus. Putting in to shore was also unplanned and resulted from necessity. Then, after we anchored, there was no contrivance or deceit in the transfer to the other boat, but this too was necessary because of the rain, for the boat we were sailing in did not have a covered deck, but the one we transferred to did. I present witnesses to these facts.

[WITNESSES]

[23] When we crossed over to the other boat, we began drinking. It's clear that Herodes left the boat and did not return again, but I did not leave the boat at all that night. The next day the man was missing, and I helped in the search no less than the others; for this was as much a concern to me as to anyone. And I was responsible for a messenger being sent to Mytilene; for on my advice we decided to send him. [24] When no one else from the (roofed) boat or from those sailing with Herodes was willing to go, I was willing to send my own attendant, though surely I did not deliberately want to send someone who would inform against me. When the man could not be found in Mytilene or anywhere else and good sailing weather had returned and all the other boats were putting out to sea, I too sailed off. I present you with the witnesses to these facts.

[WITNESSES]

[25] These are the facts; now consider the conclusions that can reasonably be drawn from them.[19] First, before I left for Aenus, when the

---

[18] The small harbor was probably the modern village of Skala Sikaminias, which is about 50 kilometers from Mytilene by road.

[19] Euxitheus contrasts the facts with likelihood (*eikota*) that result, though

man was missing and these men had already heard the news, no one accused me, or else I never would have sailed away. At that moment truth and the facts were more powerful than their accusation, and also I was still there. But when I sailed away and these men conspired and contrived their plot against me, then they made their accusation. [26] They say the man died on land when I hit him on the head with a stone, but I did not leave the boat at all. And they have precise information about this, but they cannot give any plausible account of the man's disappearance. Clearly this probably happened near the harbor; the man was drunk and left the boat at night, so he probably could not control his actions, and someone wishing to lead him far away at night would not have had a plausible excuse to do so. [27] They searched for the man for two days, both in the harbor and away from it, but they could not find anyone who had seen him or any blood or any other sign of him. So should I accept their account, even though I have witnesses that I did not leave the boat? Even if I definitely left the boat, there's no reasonable explanation how the man could disappear and not be found unless he went a long way from the sea. [28] But they say he was thrown into the sea. In what boat? Clearly the boat must have come from the harbor; why wouldn't they find it? There would probably be some evidence in the boat, if a dead man was thrown overboard at night. In fact, they said they found evidence in the boat where he was drinking and then left—where they agree he did not die; but they have not found the boat from which he was thrown into the sea or any sign of it. I present you with the witnesses to these facts.

[WITNESSES]

[29] When I sailed off to Aenus, the boat on which Herodes and I were drinking reached Mytilene. The first thing they did was go on board and search the boat, and when they found the blood, they said the man had been killed there. But when this possibility was eliminated and they discovered that it was the blood of sheep,[20] they aban-

---

some narrative is embedded in the following argument and some argument in the preceding narrative.

[20] The sheep may have been sacrificed in gratitude for escaping destruction by the storm.

doned this line of argument, and instead they seized and interrogated the men[21] under torture. [30] The man they interrogated immediately said nothing bad about me, but the other they interrogated many days later, after keeping him to themselves in the interval, and they persuaded him to accuse me falsely. I present you with the witnesses to these facts.

[WITNESSES]

[31] You have heard testimony that the man was interrogated long afterwards. Now, consider carefully the nature of this interrogation.[22] In the slave's case, since they probably promised him his freedom and had the power to put an end to his suffering, he was probably persuaded to give false testimony by both factors, hope of freedom and desire for immediate release from the torture. [32] I think you know that those who are interrogated normally testify in favor of those who have most control over the interrogation and say whatever will be pleasing to them; they will benefit most in this way, especially if those they are falsely accusing don't happen to be present. If I ordered him put on the rack for not telling the truth, this alone would probably make him recant his false accusations. As it was, the interrogators calculated their own self-interest. [33] So, as long as he was hopeful of benefiting from his false accusation, he stuck to this story; but when he realized he would be put to death, then he began telling the truth and admitted that he had been persuaded by these men to lay false charges against me. [34] But neither his persistent attempts to give

---

[21] Euxitheus is (perhaps deliberately) vague about the identities of these men. Of the two mentioned in 5.30 the first is a free man, the second a slave. The free man was probably a Mytilenean of low standing (5.49n), perhaps Euxitheus' attendant (5.24); the slave cannot have belonged to Herodes, whose relatives had to purchase him (5.47), or to Euxitheus, who would never have sold them a slave who might incriminate him.

[22] Euxitheus dwells at length on alleged irregularities in the interrogation. But although strict rules applied to an interrogation that resulted from a challenge by one litigant to the other (1.6n), these rules did not apply to interrogation during a criminal investigation, especially when the slave was suspected of involvement in the crime. Nonetheless, Euxitheus' complaints may raise doubts about the prosecution's motives.

false evidence nor his subsequent statement of the truth helped him at all; they took the man and killed him. Now they base their case against me on this informer, though everyone else treats informers in just the opposite way, rewarding free men with money and slaves with their freedom. But they rewarded this informer with death, despite the entreaties of my friends that they should not kill the man before I returned. [35] Clearly they had no need for his person, only his story. If the man were alive and I carried out the same interrogation, he would provide evidence of their plotting, but now that he's dead, his absence makes it impossible to prove the truth, while his false words live on as the truth and destroy me. Call witnesses to these facts.

[WITNESSES]

[36] In my view, they should have presented the informer here in person[23] and convicted me by this means, presenting the man publicly and asking me to interrogate him, not killing him. But tell me, which of his stories are they using now? The one he told first or the later one? And which is true? When he said I did the deed or when he denied it? [37] If we consider what is likely, his later account appears truer: he lied for his own benefit, but when his lies were about to ruin him, he thought he would save himself by speaking the truth. There was no one there to defend the truth, since I was the only ally of his later true statement and I happened to be away; others were there, however, who were going to put away his earlier false statements[24] so that they could never be corrected. [38] Men who are incriminated by informers may steal them away and eliminate them, but these men arrested this informer against me and carried out their investigation and then eliminated him. Of course, if I had eliminated the man, or had refused to hand him over, or avoided some other test, they would consider these actions most significant and would treat them as important evidence against me. So now that they themselves refuse this test when my friends challenged them,[25] then surely these same actions ought to be

---

[23] Slaves did not normally appear in court themselves, though there may have been exceptions.

[24] The exact sense is unclear; this may mean "put away for safe keeping."

[25] His friends may have requested or challenged them to wait until Euxitheus' return (cf. 5.34).

evidence against them that the accusation they brought against me is false. [39] They also say that during the interrogation the fellow agreed that he helped kill the victim, but I disagree: he did not say this but only that he led the victim and me off the boat and then, after I had killed Herodes, helped pick him up and put him in the boat, and then threw him into the sea. [40] Consider this too: at first, before being put on the wheel where he faced extreme compulsion, the man was guided by the truth and cleared me of the charge; but when he was put on the wheel, he was now guided by compulsion and testified falsely against me, hoping to be released from the torture. [41] Then when the torture stopped, he stopped accusing me of any of these things, and at the end he cried out that both of us were being ruined unjustly. He was not doing this for my sake—how could he? After all, he had falsely accused me. No, he was compelled by the truth to reaffirm the truth of his first statement. [42] Furthermore, the other man—the one sailing on the same boat, who was present to the end and was with me²⁶—was subjected to the same interrogation and agreed that the first and last statements of the man were true, since he absolved me to the end. But he disagreed with the story the slave gave while on the rack, which he told under compulsion, not for the truth; for the slave said I left the boat and killed the man and that he helped me pick up the body when it was already dead, but the other said I did not leave the boat at all.

[43] Likelihood is also my ally, for I was surely not so deluded that I planned the man's murder all by myself in order to have no accomplice (for this was the only real danger for me), but then, when it was all done, I enlisted the help of witnesses and co-conspirators. [44] Furthermore, the man was killed very near the sea and the boats, or so their story goes; but wouldn't someone being killed by just one man either cry out or somehow draw the notice of people on land or in the boat? You can hear something at much greater distance at night than

---

²⁶ "The same boat" must be the boat in which Euxitheus and Herodes set out from Mytilene, but that the man "was present to the end and was with me" seems inconsistent with the fact that he was interrogated immediately (5.30) and apparently did not accompany Euxitheus to Aenus (5.52). But "was present to the end" may just mean that he was with Euxitheus until the end of the events in the harbor, whence he returned to Mytilene while Euxitheus went on to Aenus.

in the daytime, on a beach than in the city, and they say people were still awake when the man left the boat. [45] In addition, he was killed on land and put into the boat, but there was no blood or any sign of this either on land or in the boat, although he was killed and put in the boat at night. Do you really think that under such circumstances a man could scrape away the traces on land and wipe them off the boat, when even someone in full control of himself with nothing to fear and working during the day could not make them completely disappear? How likely is this, gentlemen?

[46] Consider this in particular—and don't be upset if I repeat these points several times, since I face great danger: if you decide correctly, I am saved, but if you're at all deceived by their lies, I am destroyed—so don't let anyone make you forget this: they killed the informer and did all they could to prevent his appearing before you and to make it impossible for me to take him and interrogate him when I returned, although this would have been to their advantage. [47] But no, they purchased the man who was their informer and killed him, entirely on their own, though the city did not vote for this, and the man was not the actual killer. They should have tied him up and guarded him, or released him to my friends with guarantees, or handed him over to your officials so that you could vote on him. Instead, they themselves convicted him of the man's murder and killed him. Even a city cannot inflict the death penalty without the Athenians' permission.[27] And now you ask these jurors to judge his statements, though you yourselves have already judged his deeds. [48] Even slaves who kill their masters and are caught in the act are not put to death by the victim's relatives but are delivered to the officials according to your ancestral laws. If a slave is allowed to testify against a free man in a murder case, and a master who wishes can bring a case on

---

[27] I.e., without a decision by an Athenian court. Treaties between Athens and its allies generally specified that those accused of capital crimes be tried in an Athenian court, thereby giving Athenian jurors an opportunity to vote on the case, but such provisions probably did not apply to slaves. In 1.20 the servant is turned over to officials for execution, but we do not know if this was required. The vague reference to "your ancestral laws" in 5.48 suggests that specific rules on these matters may have been lacking, and in any case, rules may have been different in Mytilene, where there were fewer Athenian officials.

behalf of his slave, and a verdict can be rendered equally for the murder of a slave and a free man, then surely it was reasonable that he should be given a trial and not be killed by you without trial. Indeed, there would be more justice if you stood trial for this than in this unlawful trial I now face.

[49] Now consider, gentlemen, the justice and likelihood in the statements of each of the tortured men. The slave gave two accounts: once he said he had done the deed, once he denied it. But the free man,[28] who was subjected to the same interrogation, hasn't yet said anything bad about me. [50] They could not persuade him by holding out promises of freedom, as they could the other. He was willing to risk suffering whatever was necessary, when he too knew where his own advantage lay: that he would stop being tortured the moment he said what they wanted. So, which is likely to be more trustworthy, the one who always gave the same account to the end, or the one who said one thing then denied it? Even without torture, those who always give the same account of the same matters are more trustworthy than those who contradict themselves. [51] Also, an equal share of the slave's statements favors each side: his assertions favor them, his denials, me; similarly, of the two men who were tortured, one said I did it, the other denied it to the end. Of course, equality favors the defendant rather than the prosecutor, since if the number of votes is equal, this helps the defendant rather than the prosecutor.[29]

[52] On the basis of this sort of interrogation, gentlemen, they say they are quite certain I killed the man. But if I had had a guilty conscience or had done any such thing, I would have gotten rid of the two men when I had the opportunity either to take them with me to Aenus or drop them off on the mainland; I wouldn't have left behind informers who knew of the crime.

[53] They say that in the boat they found a note, which I sent to Lycinus saying I killed the man. But why did I need to send a note

---

[28] There is uncertainty about this man's status. The decree of Scamandrius prohibited the torture of Athenian citizens, though it is uncertain whether it had been enacted at the time of this speech (And. 1.43n). In any case, the tortured free man was probably a Mytilenean of low status (see 5.29n).

[29] A tie vote resulted in acquittal—the so-called vote of Athena (dramatized in Aeschylus' *Eumenides*).

since it was my accomplice who carried the note? He would have given a clearer account in person of what he did, and there was no need to hide things from him. People generally use writing for messages the messenger is not supposed to know. [54] Also, someone would need to write down a very large message so the messenger would not forget it on account of its length. But this was a short message, namely, that the man was dead. Consider this point too: the note differed from the man's testimony, and the man differed from the note, for when tortured he said he himself killed him,[30] but the note, when opened, indicated that I was the killer. [55] So which should we believe? They did not find the note the first time they searched the boat, only later, for at that time they hadn't yet devised their plot; but when the first man to be tortured said nothing that incriminated me, then they dropped the note into the boat so they would have evidence for this charge against me. [56] When the note was read and the second man under torture disagreed with the note, they could not make what had been read disappear. If they had thought from the beginning they could persuade the man to testify against me, they would never have contrived the message in the note. Call my witnesses for these matters.

[WITNESSES]

[57] What motive did I have for killing the man? There was no hostility between him and me. They go so far as to say I killed the man as a favor; but who has ever done such a deed as a favor to someone else? I don't think anyone has. Anyone intending to do this must have great hatred, and it would be abundantly clear that he's plotting a crime. But there was no hostility between us. [58] Well then, did I fear for my life, thinking he might do the same to me? A person could be forced to commit this crime for such a reason. But I had no such feelings toward him. Well, was I going to get money if I killed him? No, he didn't have any. [59] Why, I could more reasonably and truthfully ascribe this motive to you, that you are trying to kill me for money, than you could ascribe it to me. And you could much more justly be convicted of homicide by my relatives, if you kill me, than I could by you and that man's relatives, for I have shown clearly your

---

[30] This seems a direct contradiction of 5.39, explainable perhaps as an attempt to confuse the jurors.

intentions against me, but you are trying to destroy me with an unclear account. [60] I tell you this, jurors, because he has no motive for
me to kill the man; so it seems I must defend not only myself but
Lycinus too and show that their charge against him is also improbable.
I can tell you that he is in the same situation as I am: there was no way
he could get money if he killed this man, and there was no danger he
could avoid if this man died. [61] Here is the best evidence that Lycinus did not want to kill him: if he had had any previous score to settle,
he had the opportunity to bring Herodes into court on a very dangerous charge and destroy him in full accordance with your laws, and in
so doing he would have served his own interest and would have earned
the gratitude of your city by pointing out his crimes; but he decided
not to and took no legal action, even though this would have been a
more honorable course.

[WITNESSES][31]

[62] Since on that occasion he let him go, do you really think that
on this occasion, when he would have to endanger both himself and
me, he hatched this plot, even though he knew that carrying it out
would lead to my banishment into exile and his banishment from all
that is sacred and holy and of the highest value among men? Moreover, if Lycinus definitely wanted to kill him (and here I adopt the
prosecution's argument) but did not want to carry out the murder
himself, would he ever have persuaded me to commit this crime instead of him? [63] Was it that I was physically able to handle this very
risky business, while he had enough money to pay me to take risks?
Surely not, for I had money, but he had none. Quite the contrary: in
all likelihood he would more readily have been persuaded by me to do
this than I by him, since when he was in default on a debt of seven
minas, he couldn't pay it, but his friends paid it for him. And this is
the best evidence that relations between Lycinus and me were not so
friendly that I would do everything he wanted: since I did not pay his

---

[31] The manuscripts indicate a break here for witnesses, but this may be an
error. There is no indication of witnesses in the text just before or after the break;
the beginning of 5.62 follows directly from the end of 5.61; and there is no evident
reason for the testimony of witnesses at this point.

debt of seven minas when he was suffering in prison, surely I did not take so great a risk as to kill a man on his account!

[64] I have demonstrated as best I can that I am not guilty of the deed, nor is he. Their strongest argument is that the man has disappeared, and perhaps you are anxious to hear about this. Now, if you want me to speculate about it, then you jurors are in the same situation, since you're not guilty of the deed any more than I am. But if we are supposed to find the truth, then I suggest they ask one of those who did it, for he would be best able to tell them. [65] In my case, since I did not do it, the fullest answer I can give is simply that I didn't do it; but the person who did do it could easily demonstrate what happened, or if not demonstrate, at least give a plausible account. Those who commit crimes also devise explanations for the crime at the same time, but it's difficult for someone who did not do it to speculate about the unknown. I think any one of you, if someone asked you about something you didn't happen to know, would just say you didn't know; then if someone told you to say more, I think you would be quite perplexed. [66] So don't put me in this quandary which even you could not easily escape from, and don't think my acquittal should depend on how well I can speculate. It should be quite enough for me to demonstrate my own innocence in the matter, and I should be judged innocent not because I am able to discover how the man disappeared or died but because I had no reason to kill him.

[67] I know from reports that in the past killers or their victims have sometimes not been found, and it would not be right if those who were with them at the time were blamed. But many men have received the blame for other people's crimes and have been put to death before the facts became clearly known. [68] For example, the murderers of your fellow-citizen Ephialtes[32] have never yet been found. Now, if someone thought that those who were with him[33] should speculate about the

---

[32] Ephialtes, a prominent associate of Pericles, was murdered in 461, probably because of the reforms he carried out in 463. *Ath. Pol.* 25.4 names a certain Aristodicus of Tanagra as the killer, but no consensus has ever been reached. The jurors would probably have accepted Euxitheus' statement that the crime was unsolved.

[33] The expression "those who were with him" could also mean "his associates," who would presumably be the least likely to kill him.

identity of his killers, and if they didn't, they should be held responsible for the murder, that would not be right for those who were with
him. Moreover, those who killed Ephialtes did not try to get rid of
the body and by so doing run the risk of exposing the crime—as the
prosecution say I did, alleging that I let no one help me with plotting
the crime but enlisted help in lifting the body. [69] Then, not long
ago[34] a young slave, not twelve years old, tried to kill his master, and
if he hadn't become frightened at the victim's cries and run off leaving
his dagger in the wound but had had the courage to remain, all the
servants in the house would have been put to death. No one would
suspect the boy would dare commit such a crime. As it was, however,
he was arrested and later confessed. And then there were your Hellenotamiae,[35] who were blamed for financial wrongdoing, although like
me now they were not guilty. They were all put to death in anger
without any deliberation, except for one. Later the facts became clear.
[70] This one man—they say his name was Sosias—had been sentenced to death but not yet executed, and when it was revealed in the
meanwhile how the money had been lost, this man was rescued by
you, the people, though he had already been delivered to the Eleven.[36]
The others had already been put to death, though they were innocent.
[71] I think you older jurors remember these events and the younger
ones have heard about them, as I have. They show how good it is to
put things to the test of time. Perhaps this question too, how Herodes
died, might become clear later. So don't wait till later to decide that
you executed me when I was innocent, but come to the right decision
sooner and not in anger or prejudice; for there could not be worse

---

[34] We know nothing of this event besides what is said here. The point seems
to be that if the boy had not panicked, he would have succeeded in the murder
and would not have been identified; even though he would presumably have been
put to death with the other servants, the crime would remain unsolved.

[35] A group of ten (later twenty) officials who oversaw the finances of the Delian
League, an alliance of cities formed in 478 to continue the defense of Greece
against Persia. Mytilene was an important member of this alliance, which Athens
led in the Peloponnesian War against Sparta and its allies (434–404). This epi-
sode, which is not mentioned in any other source, probably occurred in the 450s
or 440s.

[36] For the Eleven, see Introduction to Ant. 5, n.1.

advisers than these. [72] It is impossible for an angry man to make good decisions, for his anger destroys the faculty he uses in planning, his judgment. Day succeeding day is a great thing, gentlemen, for restoring judgment in place of anger and for discovering the truth of what happened. [73] You can be quite certain that I deserve pity from you rather than punishment. It's reasonable to punish criminals but to pity those who are unjustly in danger, and your power to save me justly should always be stronger than my enemies' desire to destroy me unjustly. By delaying you'll still be able to do the terrible things the prosecution request, but by acting immediately you'll leave no opportunity at all for correct deliberation.

[74] Now I must also defend my father, even though it would be more reasonable for him to defend me, since he's my father. He's much older than my affairs are, but I'm much younger than his.[37] Of course, if I were giving evidence against the prosecutor here concerning a matter I wasn't certain about but knew only from hearsay, he would say I was treating him terribly. [75] But he doesn't think it's terrible to compel me to defend myself on matters that are much older than I and that I know only by word of mouth. Nevertheless, I will tell you as much as I know so my father will not be unjustly maligned before you. I might perhaps slip up and not give a completely correct account of everything he did so correctly, but that's a risk I must take. [76] Before the revolt of Mytilene[38] he showed his loyalty to you by his actions; but when the whole city wrongly decided to revolt and failed to meet your expectations, he was compelled to join with the whole city in that failure. Even during these events his feelings toward you remained the same, but he could no longer demonstrate the same loyalty, since he could not easily leave the city. His children and his property held him there like bonds, and while he remained there, it was impossible for him to act with confidence. [77] But ever since you punished the leaders of the revolt, which clearly did not include my father, and allowed the rest of the Mytileneans to live on their own land without reprisal, my father has not done anything wrong. He's done

---

[37] The sense of this puzzling sentence is clarified in 5.75.

[38] In 427 BC (see Introduction). In the following account "you" (i.e., "you jurors") pointedly suggests also "you Athenians."

everything required of him and has not neglected any of the special needs of either city, yours or Mytilene, but he has sponsored choral productions[39] and paid his taxes. [78] If he likes to live in Aenus, his intent is not to avoid any of his obligations to the city. He hasn't become a citizen of any other state as I see others doing, some going to the mainland to live among your enemies while others bring suits against you under treaties, and he's not trying to avoid your courts; his only reason is that, like you, he hates sykophants.[40] [79] It isn't right for my father to be punished as an individual for things he did together with the whole city under compulsion, not by choice. All Mytileneans will remember forever the mistake they made then. They exchanged great happiness for great misery and saw their own homeland devastated. Don't believe the slanderous charges these men have leveled against my father personally; for they have contrived this whole case against us for the sake of money. Many factors help those who want to get hold of other people's property; he's too old to assist me, and I'm much too young to be able to protect myself as I should. [80] Help me, then, and don't teach these sykophants to be more powerful than you are. If they come to you and get what they want, the lesson will be that people should come to an agreement with them and avoid your court; but if they come to you and are judged to be scoundrels who will get nothing, then honor and power will be yours, and justice will be done. Help me, then, and help justice too.

[81] You have now heard everything that can be demonstrated by human evidence and witnesses; but before casting your vote you should also look just as much to the evidence of signs from the gods. You rely on these especially in managing the public affairs of the city safely, in times of danger and other times too; [82] you should also consider these signs important and reliable in private affairs. I think you know that before now many who have embarked on a ship with unclean hands or with some other pollution have themselves perished together with others who led devout lives and fulfilled all their obli-

---

[39] Sponsoring a choral production was one of the most costly of the special liturgies required of rich Athenians; see Series Introduction.

[40] For the accusation of sykophancy, see Series Introduction.

gations to the gods.[41] Others who did not perish were subjected to life-threatening dangers because of such people. And many others attending sacrifices were shown to be unholy and were prevented from completing the proper rites. [83] With me, however, it's just the opposite in every case. Those I sailed with have enjoyed the finest voyage, and at the sacrificial rites I have attended, the sacrifice has never been anything but the finest. I think this is important evidence that the prosecution's accusations against me are untrue. Witnesses please.

[WITNESSES]

[84] I also know this, gentlemen of the jury, that if witnesses were giving testimony against me that something unholy had happened on a ship or at a sacrifice when I was present, they would consider this very strong evidence and would display these signs from the gods as clear proof of their accusation; but now that the evidence goes against their claims and the witnesses testify that my case is true and their accusation is false, now they say you should not trust the witnesses, but you should trust their arguments. Well, other men test arguments (*logoi*) against the facts (*erga*), but these men are trying to use their arguments to make you disbelieve the facts.

[85] I have now answered as many of the charges as I can remember, and I ask you to acquit me. For me acquittal means salvation; for you it is right and in accord with your oath, for you swore to judge the case according to the laws. And though no longer subject to the law under which I was arrested, I can still be tried lawfully by the proper procedure for this charge. If this results in two trials instead of one, it's the prosecutor's fault, not mine. So just because my worst enemies subject me to two trials, surely you impartial arbiters of justice will not prematurely convict me of homicide in this trial. [86] Don't do this, gentlemen; but give time a chance, for time lets those who wish discover the precise facts most accurately. I should think, gentlemen, that in such matters a trial should be held according to the laws, while according to justice the case should be tested as often as possible. In

---

[41] For the idea that the killer's pollution can affect others, see the Introduction to the Tetralogies, where discussion of pollution plays a larger role.

this way you would reach a better decision, for repeated trials are the ally of truth and the enemy of slander. [87] In a homicide case the verdict, even if wrong, overpowers justice and truth, and if you convict me, I am forced by necessity to submit to justice and the law even if I am not the murderer and have no responsibility for the crime. No one would dare disobey a verdict rendered in court just because he was confident of his own innocence, nor would he dare not submit to the law if he knew he had committed such a crime. He must yield to the verdict even if it goes against the truth, and he must yield to the truth especially if the victim has no one to avenge his death.[42] [88] For these reasons the laws, oaths, sacrifices, proclamations, and other aspects of procedure in homicide cases are very different from other cases, because it is of the highest importance to determine the facts correctly when so much is at stake. When they are decided correctly, the victim has his vengeance; but if an innocent man is convicted of murder, it is a mistake and a sin against the gods and the laws. [89] If the prosecutor brings an incorrect accusation, this is not the same as you jurors rendering an incorrect verdict. Their accusation is not final but depends on you and on the trial; but if you give an incorrect verdict in the trial, there is no way someone could undo your mistake by appealing it elsewhere. [90] How then might you decide this case correctly? By letting these men swear the established oath before presenting their case and by letting me defend myself on the issue itself.[43] And how will you do this? By acquitting me now. I won't be free of your judgment, since you'll be the ones voting on me there too.[44] If you spare me now, you'll still be able to do what you want with me then, but if you destroy me, you won't be able to deliberate about me again. [91] If you have to make a mistake, it would be more righteous to acquit someone unjustly than to destroy someone unjustly; the former is just a mistake, but the latter is also a sacrilege. When you're about to do something incurable, you need to consider it very care-

---

[42] Much of 5.87–89 is repeated in 6.4–6; see 6.4n.

[43] I.e., in a *dikē phonou*; cf. 5.10n.

[44] I.e., before the Areopagus. In fact, the jurors would be different, though there might be some overlap.

fully. It's a less serious mistake to become angry and yield to prejudice if your actions can later be remedied, since you could change and reach a correct decision later. But where there is no remedy, changing your mind and recognizing your mistake later does more harm. Some of you have already condemned someone to death and then changed your mind; but when deception leads you to change your mind, surely those who deceived you should be put to death. [92] Unintentional errors, moreover, deserve pardon, but not those that are intentional; for an unintentional error, gentlemen, happens by chance, an intentional error by choice. Now, how could there be a more intentional error than if someone immediately does what he plans to do? And killing someone with your hand or with your vote has the same effect. [93] You can be quite certain I would never have come to this city if such a crime had been on my conscience. But I came trusting in justice, and there is nothing more valuable for a man on trial than knowing he has done nothing wrong and has not sinned against the gods. In such a situation even when the body gives up, it can be rescued by a spirit that has a clean conscience and will endure anything. But a guilty conscience in itself is your worst enemy; your body is still strong but your spirit leaves, assuming this bad conscience is punishment for the crime. I come before you with no such guilt on my conscience. [94] That the prosecution are slandering me is hardly surprising; that's their business. But it's your business not to be persuaded to do what's wrong. If you believe me, you can still change your minds and cure your mistake by punishing me the second time; but there is no cure if you believe them and do what they want. It's just a short time until you can legally do what the prosecution are trying to persuade you to do illegally by your verdict. The matter requires proper deliberation, not haste. In this case you are just fact finders; next time you will be judges of the witnesses; now you just have opinions; then you will judge the truth. [95] It is the easiest thing to give false testimony against a man on trial for murder. If they persuade you just for the moment to sentence him to death, he loses his life and any possibility of revenge. Even friends will not seek revenge for someone who is dead, and if they want to, what good will it do the dead man? [96] So, acquit me now. These men will then swear the customary oath and prosecute me by the regular procedure for homicide. You will judge me by the established laws; and if I come to any harm, I can no longer argue that I'm being ruined illegally. That is my request; I have not overlooked your piety, and I am not depriving myself of justice; my salvation too lies in your oath. Put your trust in whichever of these you will, and acquit me.

6. ON THE CHORUS BOY

The speech *On the Chorus Boy* was delivered by an unknown Athenian who in 419[1] was assigned the important (and expensive) public duty or liturgy (2.2.12n) of training a boys' chorus to compete at the Thargelia, a festival held in the late Spring. This Choregus ("chorus producer") recruited the fifty boys needed for the chorus representing two of the ten tribes and provided room in his house for them to train. Being busy with his other affairs (so he tells us), he assigned the duty of training the boys to his son-in-law and three other men. One day during his absence a boy named Diodotus was given a drug to drink, perhaps to remedy a sore throat. Instead it caused his death. Two days later the boy's brother Philocrates formally charged the Choregus with unintentional homicide—specifically with "having killed the boy by planning his death" (6.16)[2]—but the Basileus,[3] the official who supervised homicide cases, refused to accept the suit. Almost two months later a new Basileus took office, and Philocrates submitted his case to this official about six weeks after that. This time it was accepted, leading to a trial at the Palladium, the court that heard cases of unintentional homicide. The penalty for unintentional homicide was exile (cf. Introduction to Ant. 3).

The Choregus advances three main lines of argument: (1) he did everything required of him and more in overseeing the chorus' training; (2) he had nothing to do with Diodotus' death and was not even

---

[1] For the date, see 6.45n.
[2] For this paradoxical charge, see below.
[3] For the Basileus, see Series Introduction.

present when he died; (3) the prosecutor only brought this case because he was bribed by the Choregus' political enemies, whose motive was to force him to abandon his own legal attacks on them. The details and supporting arguments provided in the speech suggest that all three points may be valid; nonetheless, the prosecution could attack these claims in a number of ways, and their main arguments probably focused on some different issues. We may speculate that for argument 1 they criticized the Choregus for not supervising the training himself and perhaps presented some evidence of specific faults or shortcomings in the arrangements or the people assigned to supervise the boys; for argument 2 they probably did not challenge the Choregus' claim that he was not present at Diodotus' death, since this fact could easily have been proved, but they presumably argued that as Choregus, he was responsible nonetheless, and they may have alleged that he told others to give the boy a drug; for argument 3 they may have argued that the Choregus aggressively initiated all the litigation and forced them to counter-sue in self-defense.

The charge of "planning an unintentional homicide" on the surface seems self-contradictory. As early as Draco, the planner was considered just as responsible legally for a homicide as the actual killer, but this provision was probably intended and used primarily, if not solely, for the planner of an intentional homicide. Antiphon 6 is the only case we know where the charge is planning an unintentional homicide. Presumably this designates some degree of involvement in an accidental death, but any attempt to determine the precise meaning of the charge or to set clear guidelines for its use is futile. We do not know, and the Athenians themselves probably could not say, whether someone was considered legally liable for the actions of his subordinates. Rules for such cases could only be inferred from regular practice, not from the outcome (if we knew it) of one or two cases. Athenian law allowed considerable leeway in adapting existing procedures to different circumstances (as we see in Ant. 5), and a strict or "narrow" interpretation of a statute would be difficult in any case, given the generality of the language of Athenian statutes. All we can say is that in this case the charge of planning an unintentional homicide was plausible enough for a Basileus to allow the case to proceed, and the Choregus takes the accusation seriously and does not question the legitimacy of the charge.

On the other hand, not much weight should be put on the fact that the first Basileus refused the case or that the second Basileus accepted it. The Basileus' legal duties were administrative and probably included making the initial proclamation, arranging the trial, holding preliminary hearings (*prodikasiai*), running the trial itself, and perhaps declaring the verdict (*Ath. Pol.* 57). When Philocrates first presented his accusation, the Basileus rejected it on the ground that it was necessary to hold three *prodikasiai* in three different months (6.41–42) and that his term of office would end in less than two months. Philocrates protested but did not accuse the Basileus of misconduct at the formal assessment hearing which every official underwent at the end of his term. Six weeks into the next year Philocrates presented the case again, and the new Basileus accepted it. The first Basileus probably had the legal right to reject the case, but it is not clear that he was required to reject it; the law may have said only that three *prodikasiai* were required, not that they needed to be held by the same Basileus. It is not impossible that he rejected the charge out of political friendship with the Choregus, as the prosecution probably argued, but his authority in this regard was clearly limited, and the second Basileus probably had no choice but to accept the case.[4]

Each side may have presented a strong case. The prosecution's attempt to make the Choregus responsible for the death might be loosely compared (to use a modern analogy) to a parent's attempt to hold the owner of a day-care center responsible for the death of a child at the center even if the owner was out of town that day and the drug was given by an employee without the owner's knowledge. If the owner could be depicted as irresponsible, the case might succeed. Moreover, if the Choregus' picture of this case as part of a series of suits and counter-suits is accurate, it may have mattered little to the prosecution if their chances of securing a conviction were small; the accusation in itself would have the desired effect of forcing the Choregus to withdraw from the case he was about to bring against his opponents.

In his defense the Choregus presents strong arguments on all three of his main points, and the jurors might well wonder whether someone who had taken such thorough precautions to ensure that the boys

---

[4] See further 6.42n.

would be well cared for and was not even in the house at the time could be held liable for an accidental death. The picture he paints of his opponents' political opportunism and Philocrates' vacillation, moreover, would raise strong doubts about whether this case should have been brought in the first place. All in all, the speech appears to be an effective response to the challenge of a novel and complex situation.

The prologue (1–6) is followed by a preliminary attack on the prosecution (7–10). The narration of events leading up to the death (11–14) leads to arguments that the Choregus is not responsible for it (15–19), which is followed by a further narrative (20–22) and by the Choregus' challenge that the prosecution interrogate his slaves (23–32). Narrative and argument are then mixed together in the discussion of the first Basileus' rejection of the case and Philocrates' second, successful attempt to prosecute (33–50). A very brief epilogue (51) concludes the speech.

6

[1] The sweetest thing a human being could have is a life free of danger to his person; that's what he would pray for in his prayers. If forced to confront danger, I think the best thing is a clear conscience that one has done nothing wrong. But if some misfortune should actually occur, one would hope it resulted from chance, not crime, without wickedness or shame. [2] Everyone would agree[5] in praising the laws governing these matters as the finest and most righteous of laws. They are the oldest established laws in this land and have always remained the same, which is the best sign of well-enacted laws, for time and experience teach people the faults in things. Therefore, you should not learn from the prosecutor's words whether the laws are good or not, but rather let the laws instruct you whether or not the prosecutor's words present a correct legal account. [3] This trial is of greatest importance for me, the defendant and the one facing danger. But I think it's also important for you, the jurors, to decide homicide cases correctly both for your own sake and especially out of respect for

---

[5] Cf. the nearly identical section, 5.14 (with note).

the gods. Only one verdict is given in such cases,[6] and if it is wrong,[7] it overpowers justice and truth. [4] When you convict someone, even if he is not the murderer and has no responsibility for the crime, he is forced to submit to justice, and he is banned from the city, its shrines, its trials, and its sacrifices—those greatest and most ancient of human institutions. Indeed, the law has such power that even if someone kills a person under his control and there is no one to avenge his death, from fear of the gods and human custom he purifies himself and stays away from the places mentioned in the law, hoping thus to have the best future.[8] [5] For the greater part of life for humans depends on hope, and dishonoring the gods or violating their laws deprives a person of that very hope, the greatest good humans have. No one would dare disobey a verdict rendered in court just because he was confident of his own innocence, nor would he dare not submit to the law if he knew he had committed such a crime. He must yield to the verdict even if it goes against the truth, and he must yield to the truth especially if the victim has no one to avenge his death. [6] For these reasons the laws, oaths, sacrifices, proclamations, and aspects of procedure in homicide cases are very different from other cases, because it is of the highest importance to determine the facts correctly when so much is at stake. When they are decided correctly, the victim has his vengeance; but if an innocent man is convicted of murder, it is a mistake and a sin against the gods and the laws. If the prosecutor brings an incorrect accusation, this is not the same as you jurors rendering an incorrect verdict. Their accusation is not now final, but depends on you and on the trial; but if you give an incorrect verdict in the trial, there is no way to escape the blame by assigning it elsewhere.

---

[6]This is perhaps a reference to "assessable" cases (5.10n), where the jurors take a second vote to decide the penalty.

[7]Much of the text from here to the end of 6.6 also occurs in 5.87–89; there are significant differences, however, indicating that the thought has been specifically adapted to the context of 6.3–6.

[8]If an Athenian killed a slave, the slave's master would normally take action, but if he killed his own slave there would be no one to bring suit and (apparently) there would therefore be no legal consequences. We may doubt that everyone in such circumstances behaved as Antiphon recommends.

[7] I have a rather different idea about my defense than the prosecution does about their case. They say they are prosecuting for piety and justice, but in fact their entire prosecution has been aimed at slander and deception. This is the most serious violation of justice in human affairs. They don't want to prove that I did something wrong so they can punish me with justice, but only to slander me, even if I have done nothing wrong so that they may punish me with exile from this land. [8] My view, however, is that I should first be judged on the specific charge and recount for you all that happened in connection with it; then, if you like, I'll willingly defend myself against all their other accusations, for I think these will benefit me and my reputation and will cast shame on those who accuse and slander me. [9] It's a terrible thing indeed, gentlemen: if I had done any wrong to the city in training the chorus or in anything else, they had the opportunity to make this known and prove it, punishing one of their own enemies and helping the city at the same time, but none of them was ever able to prove that I had committed any crime, large or small, against you, the people; on the other hand, in this trial, when they are prosecuting me for homicide and the law requires them to stick to the crime itself,[9] they are conspiring against me by inventing falsehoods and slandering me for my public activities. For the city, if it really has been injured, they offer an accusation but no punishment, but for themselves they think they should get private satisfaction for wrongs they say were done to the city. [10] For these accusations they don't deserve to be thanked or trusted: they are not earning the city's thanks by prosecuting a crime for which the city would gain satisfaction, if it had been wronged; and he surely does not deserve your trust, but rather your disbelief, when in a case like this he directs his accusation to charges other than those that are the subject of his prosecution. I am fairly certain you would not convict or acquit someone for any reason other than the crime itself, which is the only way consistent with righteousness and justice. Having said all that, I will begin.

[11] When I was appointed Choregus for the Thargelia[10] and was

---

[9] See 5.11n.

[10] A festival honoring Apollo on days 6 and 7 of the month Thargelion, the next to last month in the Attic year (roughly equivalent to May). Five choruses of

allotted the poet Pantacles and the tribe Cecropis in addition to my own, I performed my duties in the best and fairest way I could. First I equipped the most suitable room in my house as a training room, the same one I used when I was Choregus for the Dionysia.[11] Then I gathered the best group of boys I could without levying any fines or forcing anyone to provide guarantees[12] and without making any enemies; everything was done in the most pleasant and most suitable way possible for both of us, I making my requests and they sending their sons of their own free will. [12] When the boys first arrived I did not have the time to be there and attend to matters, for I happened to be engaged in a legal action against Aristion and Philinus,[13] and as it was an impeachment (*eisangelia*),[14] I considered it very important to prove the case to the Council and the Athenian people correctly and fairly. Since I was giving this case my full attention, I put Phanostratus in charge of whatever might be needed for the chorus. He is from the same deme as these prosecutors and a relative of mine (he married my daughter), and I thought he would give the best supervision. [13] I also appointed two others, Ameinias, from the Erechtheid tribe—I thought him a fine man, and the tribal leaders had selected him each time to collect and supervise choruses—and the other man from the

---

boys and five of men competed, each representing two of the ten Attic tribes. The speaker could recruit boys from either his own (the Erechtheid) or the Cecropid tribe. Each chorus was given a poet to compose the hymn it would sing at the festival.

[11] The most important annual festival where most tragedies and comedies were first performed. The speaker is clearly a man of wealth and importance, who regularly undertakes these costly liturgies.

[12] A Choregus could require a boy to serve in the chorus and could fine a parent who would not let his child serve unless he had a valid excuse, in which case the parent was required to post surety, which would be forfeited if the excuse proved invalid.

[13] This may be the Aristion who was Archon in 421/0. Philinus was a fairly important political figure; Antiphon wrote a speech for a case against him, of which only a few words survive.

[14] The special procedure of *eisangelia* was used for political cases such as treason; *eisangelia* cases were heard by the Council (as here) or the Assembly.

Cecropid tribe;[15] he too used to recruit choruses each time from that tribe. I also appointed a fourth man, Philippus, who was in charge of purchasing whatever the poet or anyone else might want so that the boys might receive the best training and not lack anything just because I was busy. [14] These were my arrangements for the chorus. And if I am lying to justify my behavior, the prosecution can refute me in their second speech on any point they wish. But this is the situation, gentlemen; many of these onlookers[16] have precise knowledge of all that happened, and they listened to the administrator of oaths and are paying attention to my defense. In their eyes I should like to appear true to my oath and truthful in persuading you to acquit me.

[15] I will first show you that I did not order the boy to drink the drug, I did not force him to drink, I did not give him the drink, and I was not even present when he drank. And I'm not emphasizing these points in order to absolve myself and put the blame on someone else.[17] No, I blame no one, except fortune,[18] who I think is also to blame for the deaths of many others, and whose course no one, not I or anyone else, could alter from what it must be for each of us.

[WITNESSES]

[16] You have heard the witnesses testify to the facts, gentlemen, as I promised you. From these you must examine what each side swore

---

[15] This third man is not named; either his name was not significant or it has dropped out of our manuscripts. None of these assistants is known to us.

[16] Since the Choregus was a well-known public figure, his trial would presumably attract a large crowd, including some who were present at the time of the death. Some of the jurors may also have had direct or second-hand knowledge of the events, but this would not prevent them from serving.

[17] It appears that none of the subordinates were prosecuted for homicide. Blaming someone else might have helped the speaker's case, but it would surely hurt his standing in the community if he helped convict an associate of homicide.

[18] Contrast the attitude toward fortune in the Second Tetralogy, where the defendant avoids blaming fortune, while the plaintiff argues (3.3.8) that even if the death was caused by fortune, the blame still falls to the accused. The difference may be that the defendant in that case was directly involved in the boy's death and so could be held responsible even for an accident; the Choregus may have been less inclined to blame fortune if he had given the drink himself.

and decide which of us was more truthful and swore more correctly. They swore[19] that I killed Diodotus by planning his death,[20] but I swore I did not kill him either by my own hand or by planning. [17] They base their accusation on the argument that whoever ordered the boy to drink the drug or forced him to drink or gave it to him is responsible; but I will use this same argument to show that I am not liable to the charge, since I did not order or give or force. And I will add to these that I was not present when he drank it. So, if they say it's a crime if someone orders, I did nothing wrong, for I gave no order. And if they say it's a crime if someone forces, I did nothing wrong, for I used no force. And if they say that someone who gives the drug is responsible, then I'm not responsible, for I did not give anything. [18] Anyone who wants can make accusations and level false charges, for these things are in each person's control. But I don't think their words can make it so that something happened that did not happen, or that someone committed a crime who did not, but these depend on justice and truth. Now when a murder is planned in secret[21] and there are no witnesses, you are forced to reach a verdict about the case on the basis of the prosecutor's and defendant's words alone; you must be suspicious and examine their accounts in detail, and your vote will necessarily be cast on the basis of likelihood rather than clear knowledge. [19] But here, in the first place the prosecution themselves admit that the boy's death did not result from any intent or design, and second, the entire event occurred openly in front of many witnesses, men and boys, free and slave, who would have made it very clear if anyone had committed a crime and would have provided a sure test if someone should accuse an innocent man.

[20] It is worth considering two things, gentlemen, my opponents' motives and the way they have handled this matter. From the beginning their behavior toward me has been completely different from mine toward them. [21] On the day of the boy's funeral, Philocrates

---

[19] These oaths would be sworn at a preliminary hearing and would contain each side's case in a nutshell. Thus a litigant could quote the precise words of an oath in his prepared text.

[20] For the notion of "planning," see Introduction.

[21] For this point, cf. 2.1.1–3.

here came to the court of the Thesmothetae[22] and said that I had killed his brother while he was in the chorus by forcing him to drink a drug. When he said this, I went to the court and told the same jurors that by accusing and slandering me in court Philocrates was using the law unjustly to protect certain people. I intended to bring legal action against Aristion and Philinus the next day and the day after,[23] and this was the reason he was making these statements. [22] It was easy to prove that his accusations and slanders were lies, since a great many people knew the facts—slave and free, young and old, more than fifty in all, who knew what had been said about the drinking of the drug and everything else that was said and done.

[23] I said this in court, and also issued him a challenge[24] then and there, and again the next day before the same jurors. I told him he should go and question those who had been present (and I named each one of them) taking with him as many witnesses as he wanted. He should examine the free men in a manner befitting free men,[25] for they would give a true account of what had happened for their own sake and for justice; and he should also examine the slaves, if he thought they were answering truthfully. If not, I was ready to hand over all my slaves for examination under torture, and if he wanted any slaves belonging to someone else, I agreed to get their master's permission to allow him to interrogate them however he wanted. [24] I issued this challenge openly in the court, where the jurors and many other private citizens were present as witnesses, but they were unwilling to accept this just procedure either right then and there or any time since. They are well aware that this test would not provide sup-

---

[22] The Thesmothetae presided over a variety of cases (*Ath. Pol.* 59). The Choregus' *eisangelia* (6.12n) against Aristion *et al.* was presented to the Council, but important cases were often referred to the courts, since the maximum penalty the Council could levy was a fine of 500 drachmas. The official name of this court ("the court of the Thesmothetae") is found in inscriptions as early as 446/5.

[23] The case involved several defendants, and according to Athenian law each had to be tried separately. The trial of all the generals together after the battle of Arginusae in 406 was a notorious violation of this rule; see Xen., *Hellenica* 1.7 (cf. Plato, *Apology* 32b).

[24] For the challenge to interrogation under torture (*basanos*), see 1.6n.

[25] I.e., without using torture.

port for their case against me but for my case against them, since their accusation was both unjust and untrue. [25] You know, gentlemen, that compulsion is the greatest and strongest force in human life, and proofs derived from it are the clearest and most reliable guide to justice when there are many free men and slaves who know the facts. Then you can compel the free men to tell the truth by means of oaths and pledges, which have the greatest importance for free men, and you can use a different compulsion on slaves, which will compel them to tell the truth even if their information will lead to their death, for an immediate compulsion has more effect on everyone than one in the future. [26] I challenged them on all these matters, so that every means we humans have of learning truth and justice were available to them, and they had no excuse left. In other words, I, the one who was accused and committed a crime, as they say—I was ready to provide them with the most just confirmation of the case against me; but they, the ones who make this accusation and claim they have been wronged—they were unwilling to prove they had been wronged.

[27] Now,[26] if I had refused to reveal who was present when they issued me a challenge, or to hand over servants when they asked for them, or had rejected any other challenge, they would treat these refusals as very strong evidence that the charge against me was true. So when I issued a challenge and they were the ones avoiding the test, surely it is only fair that this same refusal be evidence on my side, that the charge they are bringing against me is not true. [28] I also know this, gentlemen, that if the witnesses[27] who were present were giving testimony on their side against me, they would consider this very strong evidence, and they would display the testimony of these witnesses against me as clear confirmation of their case. But when these same witnesses testify that what I say is true and what they say is not true, they now tell you not to trust the witnesses who are testifying and say you should trust the arguments they make instead, though if I made such arguments without witnesses, they would accuse me of lying. [29] It's strange if the same witnesses should be trustworthy

---

[26] For the "hypothetical role-reversal" in 6.27–28, see 1.11n.

[27] I.e., the free witnesses. Much of the wording in this section is similar or identical to 5.84.

when they're testifying on their side but untrustworthy when testifying on my side. If no witnesses at all had been present and yet I were presenting witnesses, or if I were not presenting the witnesses who had been present but others instead, then these men's words would likely be more trustworthy than my witnesses. But when they agree that witnesses were present, and I am presenting those who were present, and from the first day both I and the witnesses have clearly been saying just what we are now saying to you, what other means than this, gentlemen, can I use to make you believe what's true and not believe what's not true?

[30] If someone should tell you with words what happened without presenting any witnesses, you would say his words are in need of witnesses; and if someone should present witnesses without providing any arguments in support of the witnesses, you could make the same objection, if you wanted. [31] But I am now presenting you with a plausible account, with witnesses who support this account, with facts supporting the witnesses, and with arguments derived from these very facts, and in addition to all this, with my two greatest and strongest arguments: the prosecutors, who are refuted by themselves and by me, and I myself, who am acquitted by them and by myself. [32] For when I was willing to be tested concerning their accusation but they were not, then they did wrong, and they absolved me, surely, for they became witnesses testifying against themselves that their accusation was both unjust and untrue. So, if I have presented my opponents themselves as witnesses in addition to my own witnesses, what other evidence or what arguments could I possibly introduce to show that I am acquitted of the charge?

[33] From what has been said and demonstrated, I think it only right that you should acquit me, knowing that nothing in this accusation concerns me. But to give you an even better understanding of the case, I'll add a few words to show you that the prosecutors are the most perjured and unrighteous of men. Because of this case they deserve not just my hatred but the hatred of all of you and the rest of the citizens. [34] I say this because on the first day, when the boy died, and on the following day when his body was laid out, they did not think to accuse me of any crime whatsoever in this affair, but they spent time talking with me. On the third day, however, the day of the

boy's funeral, they were persuaded[28] by my enemies, and they prepared an accusation and a proclamation banning me from the places prescribed in the law.[29] Who persuaded them? And why were they so eager to persuade them? I must explain this to you. [35] I was about to go to trial before the Council in my impeachment case against Aristion, Philinus, Ampelinus,[30] and the scribe of the Thesmothetae, who was their partner in embezzlement. Given the facts in the case and the seriousness of their crimes, they had no hope of acquittal, but they thought if they could persuade these men to register their case and make a proclamation banning me from the places prescribed in the law, this would make them safe, and they would be rid of the whole affair. [36] For the law says that when someone is inscribed as the accused in a homicide case, he is banned from the places prescribed in the law; and I would not be able to proceed with my prosecution if I was banned from the places prescribed in the law, while they would easily be acquitted and would pay no penalty to you for their crimes, since I was the one who had brought the impeachment and knew the facts, and I would no longer be prosecuting them. I was not the first person Philinus and the others used this scheme against; they also used it against Lysistratus[31] earlier, as you yourselves have heard.

[37] Thus, they were anxious to register me immediately, the day after the boy was buried, even before purifying the house and conducting the proper rites; for they knew that was the day set for the trial of the first of them, and they wanted to prevent me from prosecuting even one of them and revealing their crimes to the court. [38] But the

---

[28] The implication is that they were bribed, since only the victim's relatives could normally bring a homicide case; others who wanted the case brought against the Choregus would have to "persuade" the boy's relatives to do so.

[29] Although a homicide victim's relatives made a proclamation naming the killer, only the registration of the case with the Basileus, who then made his own proclamation, had the legal consequence of barring the accused from public places—and thus from other legal actions (cf. 3.1.2n).

[30] Nothing is known of Ampelinus or the scribe, who are not mentioned in earlier references to the case (6.12, 6.21).

[31] Probably the person mentioned several times in plays of Aristophanes, once as part of a group including Antiphon (*Wasps* 1302).

Basileus read them the laws and showed them that there wasn't enough time to register the case and issue all the necessary summonses;[32] and I brought those who were behind this plot to trial and convicted them all, and, as you know, they were assessed fines. When these men here found they could not give them the assistance they had originally been paid to give, at that point they approached me and my friends asking for reconciliation and saying they were ready to make amends for their mistakes. [39] My friends persuaded me to agree, and we were reconciled during the Dipolieia[33] in front of witnesses at the temple of Athena.[34] Afterwards we spent time together and talked in shrines, in the Agora, at my house, at their house, and everywhere else. [40] To top it all off, by Zeus and all the gods, in the Council-house in front of the Council Philocrates here joined me on the podium, and with his hand on my arm he talked with me, calling me by name, and I did the same. Naturally, the Council thought it pretty strange when they later learned that a proclamation banning me from the places prescribed in the law had been issued by the same people they had seen talking with me the day before.

[41] Now, pay close attention and think back, gentlemen, for not only will I prove this from witnesses, but when you hear what they did, you will easily understand that I am speaking the truth. First, they accuse the Basileus of refusing to register the suit because of my efforts, but this is evidence against them and shows they are lying. [42] After he had registered a suit, the Basileus had to hold three preliminary hearings in three months and then hold the trial in the fourth month, just as we're doing now; but he only had two months left in his term of office, Thargelion and Skirophorion.[35] Obviously he would not be able to conduct the trial during his own term, and he is not allowed to pass on a homicide case to his successor; indeed, no Basileus in this country has ever passed on a homicide case. Since he could not hold the trial or pass it on to anyone, he decided not to register the case in

---

[32] The Choregus explains this constraint in more detail below (6.42).

[33] For this festival, see 2.4.8n.

[34] The Parthenon.

[35] The last two months in the Athenian year; the term of all annual offices ended at the end of the year. Hekatombaion and Metageitnion (6.44) are the first and second months.

violation of your laws.³⁶ [43] The strongest evidence that he did them no wrong is that Philocrates here shook down and blackmailed other officials when they presented their accounts, but despite accusing the Basileus of terrible crimes, he brought no charges against him during his accounting.³⁷ What stronger evidence could I present that Philocrates was not wronged by me or the Basileus? [44] When this present Basileus took office on the first day of the month of Hekatombaion, they could have registered the case on any day they wanted, thirty days in all, but they never did. Then in the month of Metageitnion they could also have registered the case on any day they wanted from the beginning, but they still did not register it but passed up twenty days of this month. Thus, they had more than fifty days³⁸ under this Basileus in which to register the case but did not. [45] Anyone else who cannot proceed with the same Basileus because of the time limit ⟨registers³⁹ his case as soon as the new Basileus takes office.⟩ But these men knew the law well and saw me entering the Council-house as a Councilor—and in the Council-house there stands a shrine to Zeus of the Council and Athena of the Council, and the Councilors go and pray in it, and I was one of the ones who did this, and I entered all the other shrines with the Council, and I sacrificed and prayed on behalf of this city; and furthermore, I served as a member of the first Prytany⁴⁰ for all but two days, supervising the sacred rites and offering

---

³⁶ The Choregus' language is carefully crafted to suggest that legally the Basileus had no other choice, but the specific evidence is not as conclusive as he claims, and the Basileus may have had some discretion in the matter.

³⁷ The accounting (*euthynai*) that Athenian officials had to submit to at the end of their term in office could be challenged by any citizen. This presented an opportunity for aggressive prosecution of one's political enemies or malicious threats of prosecution in the hope of a financial settlement. It may seem significant that Philocrates did not lodge a protest at the Basileus' hearing, but at that time he and the Choregus had apparently been reconciled.

³⁸ Since thirty and twenty add up to exactly fifty, either "more than fifty" is a simple exaggeration or the text is corrupt.

³⁹ Something is clearly missing from this sentence in the text preserved in our manuscripts; the sense given here seems required by the context.

⁴⁰ The Choregus had been selected by lot to be a member of the Council for that year. The Council comprised 50 men from each of the ten tribes; its year was

sacrifices for the democracy, and I directed the voting on issues and stated my views on the highest and most important public matters, and all this was done in public view. [46] These men were in town and present at these events; they could have registered the case and banned me from all these events, but they decided not to. Surely if they had really been wronged, it was a serious enough matter that they would remember and be concerned about it, for their own sake as well as the city. Then why didn't they register it? Why were they spending time talking with me? They were spending time with me because they didn't think I was a murderer, and they did not register the case for the same reason, that they didn't think I had killed the boy or was liable for a charge of homicide, or that I had anything to do with the matter.

[47] How could people be more wicked or have less regard for the law than these men, who think they can persuade you of something when they cannot persuade themselves, and who ask you to convict when their own actions have spoken for acquittal? Other men test arguments against the facts, but these men are trying to use their arguments to make you disbelieve the facts. [48] If I have not said or shown you anything else, and if I have presented no witnesses but have only demonstrated this, that when they were getting money to attack me they leveled charges and made a proclamation,⁴¹ but when no one was giving them money they spent time talking with me, this in itself would be sufficient to make you acquit me and judge them the most perjured and unrighteous of all men. [49] These men! Is there any litigation they would not bring to court, is there any court they would not try to deceive, is there any oath they would hesitate to transgress? After all, they took thirty minas from the Revenue Managers, the Su-

---

divided into ten Prytanies of 36 or 37 days each, each tribe holding the Prytany once each year. The tribe holding the Prytany carried out all the administrative duties of the Council. This year the Choregus' tribe was assigned the first Prytany, which at the time was always 37 days long. He tells us he served 35 of these days ("all but two") and earlier (6.44) that he served for 20 days of Metageitnion (the second month). We can thus calculate that the new Council began its service that year on the 16th day of Hekatombaion (the first month), and the evidence of inscriptions informs us that this happened in 419/8 BC and in no other year near this.

⁴¹ I.e., naming the (alleged) killer (6.28).

pervisors of Public Resources, the Debt Collectors,[42] and the secretaries who work for them to bring this case against me, forcing me out of the Council-house and swearing fearful oaths, all because when I was in the Prytany I had learned of terrible crimes they had committed and had brought an impeachment (*eisangelia*) against them to the Council[43] and had shown that the matter warranted investigation and prosecution. [50] Now the whole affair has been brought to light, and they and their accomplices with whom the money was deposited are paying for their crimes—crimes so outrageous that even if they wished, they could not easily deny them.

[51] Is there then no court they would not enter intent on deceiving it? Is there no oath they would hesitate to swear, these ungodly villains? They know you are the most righteous and just jurors in Greece, and yet they come before you intent on deceiving you if they can, despite the mighty oaths they have sworn.

---

[42] The *poristai*, the *pōlētai*, and the *praktores*; these all managed public funds.
[43] Cf. 6.12n.

FRAGMENT 1. ON THE REVOLUTION

After the Athenian expedition to Sicily (see the Introduction to Andocides) was defeated by Sparta and its allies in 413, turmoil in Athens led to a coup by a group of four hundred oligarchs. However, this government of the Four Hundred was soon overthrown, its chief proponent, Phrynichus, was assassinated, and almost all the other leading oligarchs went into exile. Antiphon remained in Athens, however, where he and one or two others were tried for treason. The prosecution was an *eisangelia* (6.12n) before the Council, and the specific charge concerned their participation in an embassy to Sparta near the end of the Four Hundred's brief reign. They were convicted and sentenced to death, confiscation of property, loss of burial rights, and loss of citizen rights for their descendants.

The speech Antiphon delivered at this trial was widely admired at the time: one of his readers, Thucydides, called it "the best defense in a capital case" (8.68), and Aristotle reports (*Eudemian Ethics* 3.5) that the tragedian Agathon praised it, earning Antiphon's response that the praise of one expert is worth more than that of many ordinary men. Despite this praise, the speech did not survive antiquity, and until the twentieth century it was only known from a few lines and isolated words in later authors.[1] In 1907 several pages of a badly mutilated papyrus text from the second or third century AD were discovered and were immediately identified as from this speech. The first excerpt

---

[1] These include Fragments 1b, preserved in Harpocration, and 1c, preserved in the *Suda*.

translated here (1a) is from the best-preserved part of the papyrus; the restoration of other parts is mere guesswork.[2]

Although we are still in the dark about Antiphon's overall defense strategy, these fragments convey something of his approach to the situation and the tone of his argument. Fragment 1a begins in the middle of a common argument (cf. 5.57–63) rejecting possible motives for the alleged crime of participation in an oligarchic coup; even though the specific charge concerned an embassy to Sparta, Antiphon seems to have addressed the broader accusation of participation in the coup of the Four Hundred. He then develops a positive argument from likelihood (*eikos*), that his special profession of logographer would be curtailed under an oligarchy but would thrive under a democracy. Since he could scarcely deny his evident role in the coup, he may have gone on to argue that his goal was not oligarchy but an improved democracy. Fragment 1b responds to the charge that Antiphon's grandfather was a supporter of the tyrants, and Fragment 1c seems to prepare for a refutation of the prosecution's expectation that Antiphon will use tears and supplication in his defense. There are some interesting hints at parallels with Socrates' defense (as presented in Plato's *Apology*) a dozen years later.

FRAGMENT I

[1a] ⟨What was supposed to be my motive for conspiring against the democracy? Was it⟩ that I had been selected for a public office where I had handled large sums of money and faced an accounting[3] that I feared? Had I been disfranchised? Had I done you some wrong? Did I fear an impending trial? Surely I had no such motive, since I faced none of these situations. Well, were you depriving me of property? Or ⟨was it because of⟩ wrongs done by my ancestors? . . . ⟨Others⟩ desire a different form of government from the one they have

---

[2] Another part of the papyrus preserves a few legible words, including "Theramenes, who prosecuted me. . . ." Theramenes was originally a member of the Four Hundred but later helped overthrow them; he was also a member of the Thirty in 404 (see Lys. 12.62–78).

[3] See 6.43n.

because they want to escape punishment for crimes they have committed or take revenge for what they have suffered and not suffer in return. But I had no such motive.

My accusers say I used to compose speeches for others to deliver in court and that I profited from this.[4] But under an oligarchy I would not be able to do this, whereas under a democracy I have long been the one with power because of my skill with words. I would be worthless in an oligarchy but very valuable in a democracy. Surely then it's not likely that I desire an oligarchy. Do you think I'm the only man in Athens who cannot figure this out or cannot understand what is to my own advantage?

[1b] . . . on the charges brought by Apolexis,[5] that like my grandfather I was a political partisan . . . the ancestors would not have been able to punish the tyrants but have been unable to punish their bodyguards.[6]

[1c] [The prosecutor] asked that you not pity me, since he feared that I would try to persuade you with tears and supplication.

---

[4] Philostratus reports (*Lives of the Sophists* 499) that "comedy attacks Antiphon for being clever in forensic matters and for selling for a high price speeches that run counter to justice, especially to those in great danger [of conviction]."

[5] Otherwise unknown.

[6] The argument apparently is that although Antiphon, like his grandfather, may have been on the side of those no longer in power, his grandfather was not punished for this, and so he should not be punished either.

ANDOCIDES

Translated with introduction by Douglas M. MacDowell

INTRODUCTION

Andocides was born not long before 440 BC. He was descended from a distinguished Athenian family. As a young man he became a member of a group of friends, including Euphiletus and Meletus, who shared a political interest. They held oligarchic opinions, in the sense that they disliked the Athenian democracy; they disapproved of the power of the mass of ordinary citizens in the Assembly and the demagogic politicians who led them.

In 415, during a period of peace in the middle of the Peloponnesian War between Athens and Sparta, the Athenians were preparing a great naval expedition against Syracuse in Sicily. The man who had persuaded them to undertake this was Alcibiades, the most flamboyant politician of the time. Some of them thought that they might even gain possession of the whole of Sicily. Alcibiades hoped to gain military renown for himself, and he was appointed to command the expeditionary force jointly with the cautious Nicias and the experienced Lamachus. But one day shortly before the force was due to sail from Piraeus it was found that most of the Herms in Athens had been mutilated during the night. These were the images of the god Hermes standing in streets and outside houses. Each was a quadrangular stone pillar, carved with a bearded head at the top and a phallus at the front. The mutilation alarmed many Athenians: if the god of travelers took offense at it, might he not take his revenge by wrecking the ships or creating some other disaster for the men who were about to sail to Sicily?

A determined effort was made to discover the perpetrators. While the matter was being investigated, another religious scandal came to light. The Eleusinian Mysteries were the focal point of a festival held annually in honor of Demeter and her daughter (sometimes called Kore or Persephone or Pherrephatta), "the Two Goddesses." A secret ceremony was held in the temple at Eleusis a few miles from Athens, conducted by priests who belonged to the two aristocratic families of the Eumolpidae and the Ceryces. It was believed that those who had been initiated in the ritual would enjoy a happy life after death, but they were strictly forbidden to reveal the secrets to the uninitiated. The scandal that emerged in 415 was that some men had been "doing the Mysteries" in private houses. This seems to mean that they had been acting out parodies of the secret ritual to entertain their friends, for fun rather than for any serious purpose; but the effect had been not only that religious belief was mocked, but also that the secrets of the Mysteries had been divulged to some men who had not been initiated and so were not entitled to know them.

There was panic in Athens, partly from fear of the gods and partly from fear that these audacious acts might be the prelude to a political revolution intended to subvert the democracy. Both the profanation of the Mysteries and the mutilation of the Herms gave rise to many denunciations. Some men were condemned to death; others fled from Athens to avoid trial and probable execution. Among those accused was Alcibiades, but he protested his innocence. If the mutilation was really a scheme to deter the Athenians from sending the expedition to Sicily, Alcibiades cannot have been responsible for it, but it seems that he must have participated in the profanation of the Mysteries. He was allowed to set off for Sicily; soon afterwards he was recalled to stand trial, but escaped to the Peloponnese.

Also accused were Andocides, his father Leogoras, and other members of their family. Andocides' speech *On the Mysteries* includes a vivid description of the imprisonment of himself and his relatives, and of how he agonized over the decision to reveal what he knew even though it meant betraying his friends (1.48–53). Finally he turned state's evidence on being given immunity from prosecution. He relates how he reported that the mutilation was planned and carried out by Euphiletus and other members of their group, but not by Andocides himself, who was laid up with a riding injury at the time (1.61–64). Thus he admits that he knew of the plan but denies that he actually took part in carrying it out. He also denies that he was involved in the profanation of the Mysteries, and in particular he denies that he obtained his own release by denouncing his father for it. (Attacking one's own parents was regarded by Greeks as the worst of crimes.)

Whether he was really guilty is one of the most intriguing criminal problems of the ancient world, and the evidence is not quite sufficient for solving it. The main evidence we have is his own speech, delivered about fifteen years later, but in it he is arguing for his life and we cannot take for granted that he is telling the truth. His account of the extent of his involvement in the mutilation does seem plausible, and may be cautiously accepted. His account of the profanation, on the other hand, seems to suppress some awkward facts. In particular, although he mentions four occasions when the Mysteries were profaned in private houses and gives some evidence of the men who were involved in them (1.12–18), it is notable that he does not mention another occasion of which documentary evidence is preserved by Plutarch (*Alcibiades* 22), when the Mysteries were profaned in Alcibiades' house by Alcibiades, Pulytion, and Theodorus. This arouses our suspicion that Andocides has deliberately suppressed information about that particular incident because it was one at which he himself was present. But the whole question of the guilt or innocence of Andocides in the religious scandals is too complex to be considered fully here; for detailed discussion readers should turn to the two editions of his speeches mentioned at the end of this Introduction.

The upshot in 415 was that Andocides was not condemned either for profanation of the Mysteries or for mutilation of the Herms, although he was widely suspected of being guilty of both. It was evidently in order to get at him that a decree, proposed by an otherwise unknown man named Isotimides, was passed by the Assembly. It laid down that anyone who was guilty of impiety and had confessed it should be excluded from the Agora and all sacred places. Since everyone else guilty of either the profanation or the mutilation had already been executed or had fled into exile, Andocides was probably the only person to whom the decree might be thought to apply. He bowed to this pressure and left Athens altogether. For the next few years he lived abroad, spending some of the time in Cyprus. He made two attempts to return to Athens, the second of which was the occasion of his speech *On His Return*; but both these attempts were unsuccessful.

In 404 the Peloponnesian War came to an end when Athens was besieged and beaten by Sparta. The oligarchic regime of the Thirty ruled oppressively in 404/3, but then there was civil war, and the Thirty were expelled. Democracy was restored from the year in which Eucleides was Archon (403/2), and the Athenians tried to make a fresh start. They swore an oath to observe an amnesty for what they had done to one another in the civil war. No one (except members of the Thirty and their henchmen the Eleven) was to be prosecuted for any offense committed before the Archonship of Eucleides. They authorized a review of all their laws; those which were to remain valid were inscribed on stone, and any law not so inscribed was declared invalid.

So Andocides returned to live in Athens, assuming that he would not now be penalized for his actions in 415. But three years later, probably in 400 or possibly in 399, he found himself prosecuted for infringement of the decree of Isotimides. He defended himself with his speech *On the Mysteries*, which is our principal source of information about his life. He was acquitted, and thus was able to continue living in Athens.

In 392/1 he was one of the members of an Athenian delegation sent to Sparta to discuss a treaty, and on returning home he delivered his speech *On the Peace with Sparta*, recommending acceptance of the proposed terms. But he and the other delegates were accused of corruption and had to flee Athens. Presumably he never came back again; nothing is known of his life after that.

For the first speech this translation follows the Greek text as printed in *Andokides, On the Mysteries*, edited by Douglas MacDowell (Oxford, 1962). For the other speeches it follows the text of *Greek Orators*, IV, *Andocides*, edited by Michael Edwards (Warminster, 1995). Both those editions include introductions and commentaries which may be consulted for more detailed discussion of Andocides' life and speeches. In the present translation Greek names are generally given in Latinized forms. This departure from my normal practice has been adopted to conform to the policy of the whole series of translations.

1. ON THE MYSTERIES

~~~~~~

In 403 or 402 BC Andocides returned to Athens, believing himself to be protected by the recent amnesty and revision of the legal code. But about three years later, probably in 400 or possibly in 399, he was prosecuted by *endeixis*, a legal procedure for accusing someone of exercising rights to which he was not entitled. He had attended the Eleusinian Mysteries, and the prosecution alleged that he was forbidden to do so by the decree of Isotimides. Thus the case did not technically infringe the amnesty, which applied to offenses committed before 403; although the charge depended on the impious acts which he was said to have committed in 415, the specific act for which he was being prosecuted was attendance in the temple at Eleusis in 400 (or 399). There was also a secondary charge, that he had placed an olive-branch of supplication on the altar of the Eleusinium in Athens at the time of the Mysteries, which was illegal. The penalty demanded by the prosecutors was death, but probably they hoped that he would simply leave Athens, making a trial unnecessary. However, he stood his ground, and the trial took place. We do not now have the main speech for the prosecution, but a short speech, *Against Andocides*, is preserved among the speeches of Lysias (no. 6). It is unlikely that Lysias wrote it, but it does seem to be the genuine text of one of the supporting speeches of the prosecution in the trial. Its arguments, however, are mostly in general terms and give us only a little additional information.

The speech *On the Mysteries* is the one with which Andocides defended himself. In the first half he argues that he was not guilty of impiety in 415 and had not confessed it, so that even if the decree of Isotimides were still valid, it would not apply to him. But he then goes on to argue that the amnesty and the revision of the laws in 403 have made the decree of Isotimides no longer valid. It is not clear that he is legally correct here, since the decree was not a law and thus strictly was not invalidated by the measures of 403; but it probably had been generally assumed to be obsolete, and prosecution for infringement of it in 400 was contrary to the spirit if not to the letter of the amnesty, which had been intended partly to protect men suspected of oligarchic sympathies.

In the later part of the speech he moves from defense to attack by making allegations against his prosecutors, who were Cephisius, Meletus (a different man from the Meletus who had been a comrade of Andocides in 415), Epichares, and Agyrrhius. The first three, he says, had all committed offenses before 403 themselves, so that they too are open to prosecution if they do not accept the validity of the amnesty; and Agyrrhius is acting from personal spite against Andocides as a rival in the matter of the purchase of a tax-collecting right. But the sinister figure who emerges behind all these is Callias. Callias son of Hipponicus (not to be confused with other men named Callias who are also mentioned in the speech) was a well-known member of the aristocratic family of Ceryces and himself held one of the hereditary priesthoods of the Eleusinian Mysteries. Andocides alleges that Callias wanted to get hold of a girl who was an orphaned relative both of Callias' son and of Andocides. In accordance with Athenian law of inheritance, the nearest male relative was entitled to claim her as his wife, and Andocides and his cousin Leagrus were the nearest; but Leagrus had withdrawn his claim, and if Andocides were driven out of Athens, Callias' son as the next nearest relative would be able to claim her and would then let her live with Callias. This lurid account of Callias' motives may or may not be true; we have no way of checking it. But in any case it provides some fascinating information about law and custom concerning Athenian families.

Evidently the speech had the desired effect on the jury, for we know that Andocides was acquitted. The text as we have it is not the work of an expert orator or stylist. Sometimes the wording is clumsy or repetitive. But it is the speech of a man fighting for his life, and he tells his version of the facts with force and vividness. The arrangement of topics is sufficiently clear and logical: after introductory remarks (1–

10) he first deals with the events of 415, not in chronological order but taking everything concerning the profanation of the Mysteries (11–33) before everything concerning the mutilation of the Herms (34–70); then he turns to the decree of Isotimides and the reasons why the events of 405–403 have made it no longer valid (71–91); and that leads into the attacks on the prosecutors and on the motives of Callias (92–136), including a brief but effective rebuttal of the secondary charge about the suppliant-branch (110–116). The passages of narrative are always lucid and sometimes gripping. He is clever at using snatches of dialogue to bring them to life: "We've done it, Andocides, and carried it out. As for you, if you're willing to keep quiet . . ." (63). Above all, the account of the maneuvers of Callias and his son is a masterpiece of scornful humor: "Who can he be? Oedipus? Aegisthus? Or what name should we give him?" (129). Altogether it is one of the most absorbing and effective speeches surviving from ancient times.

For more detailed discussion of Andocides' guilt or innocence, see the editions by MacDowell and Edwards (see Introduction to Andocides), and also J. L. Marr, "Andocides' Part in the Mysteries and Hermae Affairs, 415 BC," *Classical Quarterly* 21 (1971): 326–338; William D. Furley, *Andokides and the Herms: A Study of Crisis in Fifth-Century Athenian Religion* (*BICS* Supplement 65, London 1996). On the Eleusinian Mysteries, see George E. Mylonas, *Eleusis and the Eleusinian Mysteries* (Princeton, 1961); Walter Burkert, *Greek Religion* (Oxford, 1985), 285–290; Kevin Clinton, *Myth and Cult: The Iconography of the Eleusinian Mysteries* (Stockholm, 1992). On the Herms, see Robin Osborne, "The Erection and Mutilation of the Hermai," *Proceedings of the Cambridge Philological Society* 31 (1985): 47–73.

I

[1] Gentlemen: my opponents' plotting and keenness to do me harm in every way, whether justly or unjustly, ever since I first returned to Athens, are known to pretty well all of you; I don't need to speak at length about that. But I'm going to make you some fair requests. They're easy for you to grant, but worth a great deal for me to obtain from you. [2] First, I want you to bear in mind that I've come here today although nothing compelled me to remain in Athens (since

I'd neither provided sureties nor been imprisoned),[1] because I put my trust above all in justice, and also in you, believing that you would reach a just verdict and not allow me to be unjustly destroyed by my opponents, but rather would give me just protection, in accordance with your laws and with the oaths which you who will cast your votes have sworn. [3] It's reasonable for you, gentlemen, to hold the same opinion about men who face danger voluntarily as they hold about themselves. When men refuse to stay in Athens to face trial, acknowledging their guilt, you reasonably concur with their own decision; but when men have stayed here, confident of their innocence, it's right for you too to hold the same opinion as they have held about themselves, and not to judge them guilty in advance.

[4] Thus in my case, when a lot of people were informing me that my enemies were saying I wouldn't stay but would certainly get away into exile—"What would be the point of Andocides' staying for such a serious trial? He can leave here and keep all his possessions; and if he travels to Cyprus, where he's come from, he has plenty of good land offered to him, and a grant as well. So will he want to risk his own life? For what purpose? Can't he see how things are in Athens?" But in fact, gentlemen, my view is quite the opposite of this. [5] I couldn't bear to live somewhere else and keep all my property while losing my own country, even granting that the situation in Athens is as bad as my opponents say. I'd far rather be a citizen of it than of other cities which may seem to me very prosperous at present. It's because I take that view that I've entrusted my life to you.

[6] So I ask you, gentlemen, to show more sympathy to me, the defendant, than to the prosecutors, realizing that even if you give him an equal hearing, the defendant is bound to be at a disadvantage. They've brought the prosecution after putting their plot together over a long period, without any danger to themselves, whereas in making my defense I suffer from fear, danger, and the greatest prejudice against me. So it's reasonable for you to show more sympathy to me

---

[1] Normally a man prosecuted by *endeixis* (cf. 1.8n) was either imprisoned or required to provide sureties to ensure that he did not abscond before trial. The fact that Andocides' opponents did not insist on this probably means that they were hoping that he would leave Athens voluntarily.

than to the prosecutors. [7] You should also bear in mind that often before now people have made serious accusations and then have immediately been proved to be lying so plainly that you'd have been much more pleased to punish the accusers than the accused. Others have caused people to be executed undeservedly by giving false evidence, and then you have convicted them of perjury when it was no longer any use to the victims. Since that kind of thing has often happened before now, it's reasonable for you to wait before believing the prosecution's statements. Whether the accusations are serious or not can be decided from what the prosecutor has said; whether they're true or false, you can't know before you've also heard my defense.

[8] I wonder, gentlemen, where I should begin my defense: from the end of the story, explaining how they brought the indictment (*endeixis*)[2] against me illegally, or with the decree of Isotimides and how it's invalid, or with the laws and the oaths which have been taken, or should I explain the facts to you right from the beginning? My chief difficulty is this: you may not all feel equal indignation about all the accusations, but each of you may have some point on which he'd like me to defend myself first; but it's impossible to speak about everything at once. So I think it's best for me to explain all the facts to you from the beginning, leaving nothing out. If you understand correctly what happened, you'll easily realize what lies the prosecutors have told against me.

[9] To give a just verdict is, I'm sure, your intention anyway, and it was because I trusted you to do so that I stayed in Athens, seeing that in both private and public matters you attach the greatest importance to voting in accordance with your oaths (and that alone is what holds the city together, against the wishes of those who don't want it to be so). But I do ask you to give my defense a sympathetic hearing, and not to make yourselves my adversaries, nor treat my words with suspicion, nor pick on my expressions, but to listen to my defense from beginning to end, and only then vote for whatever you think is best for yourselves and most in accordance with your oaths. [10] As I said

---

[2] *Endeixis* was a prosecution procedure which involved pointing out to an official that a person had entered a place or performed an act from which he was prohibited.

to you before, gentlemen, I'll make my defense about everything from the beginning, first about the actual charge on which the indictment was based, for which I've been brought to trial today—about the Mysteries and how no impiety was committed by me, no information given, and no confession made, and I don't know whether the information that was given you about them was false or true; all this I'll explain to you.

[11] There was a meeting of the Assembly for the generals appointed to Sicily, Nicias[3] and Lamachus[4] and Alcibiades, and Lamachus' flagship was already outside the harbor. Pythonicus stood up in the Assembly and said: "Athenians, you are sending out this great armed force, and you are going to incur danger. But Alcibiades the general, as I shall prove to you, has been performing the Mysteries with others in a private house; and if you vote to give immunity[5] to the person to whom I tell you to, a servant of one of the men present here, though he is uninitiated, will tell you the Mysteries. If not, do whatever you like with me, if I'm not telling the truth." [12] Alcibiades responded at great length, denying it; and the Prytaneis[6] decided to clear the meeting of the uninitiated[7] and to go themselves to fetch the young man whom Pythonicus told them to. They went, and they brought back a servant of Alcibiades named Andromachus. After they'd voted to give him immunity, he said Mysteries were performed in Pulytion's house; Alcibiades, Nicides, and Meletus[8] were the actual performers, but others were also present and saw what was done, including some slaves—himself, his brother, Hicesius the piper, and Meletus' slave. [13] He was the first to give this information, and he listed these men.

---

[3] A leading general and politician. He usually favored peaceful policies: he was largely responsible for the Peace of Nicias made between Athens and Sparta in 421, and he initially opposed Alcibiades' proposal to send the expedition to Sicily in 415.

[4] An experienced general mocked by Aristophanes in *Acharnians*.

[5] Immunity from prosecution, for a man giving evidence for the state.

[6] The presidents of the Assembly.

[7] Those who had not been initiated into the Mysteries could not be allowed to hear the evidence, because it might reveal the secrets.

[8] Andocides' friend (1.63), not his accuser (1.94).

Polystratus was arrested and executed; the rest fled into exile, and you[9] condemned them to death. Please take the list of their names and read it out.[10]

[NAMES] *Andromachus informed against the following: Alcibiades, Nicides, Meletus, Archebiades, Archippus, Diogenes, Polystratus, Aristomenes, Oeonias, Panaetius.*

[14] That was the first information given by Andromachus against those men. Please call Diognetus.[11] Were you a commissioner of inquiry, Diognetus, when Pythonicus made his announcement in the Assembly about Alcibiades?

I was.

Do you know that Andromachus gave information about what was done in Pulytion's house?

I do.

Are those the names of the men against whom he informed?

They are.

[15] A second information was then given. There was a man named Teucer, a metic[12] in Athens. He departed secretly to Megara, and from there made an offer to the Council that, if they gave him immunity, he would give information concerning the Mysteries, being himself a participant, and about the others who performed with him, and would say what he knew about the mutilation of the Herms. The Council, which had authority to act, voted in favor, and they went to Megara to fetch him. When he was brought, having obtained immunity, he

---

[9] "You" addressed to an Athenian jury often means the Athenian people in the Assembly or in another jury, not necessarily the jurors in the present case.

[10] This sentence is addressed to the clerk of the court, who was responsible for reading documents aloud.

[11] Presumably a different Diognetus from the one denounced by Teucer soon afterwards (1.15).

[12] A metic was a free person who was not an Athenian citizen but had permission to reside permanently in Athens.

listed his companions, and they fled into exile following Teucer's information. Please take the list of their names and read it out.

[NAMES] *Teucer informed against the following: Phaedrus,*[13] *Gniphonides, Isonomus, Hephaestodorus, Cephisodorus, himself, Diognetus,*[14] *Smindyrides, Philocrates, Antiphon,*[15] *Teisarchus, Pantacles.*

Remember, gentlemen, that the truth of all this is also admitted. [16] A third information was given. The wife of Alcmeonides,[16] who was previously the wife of Damon[17] (Agariste was her name), gave information that Mysteries were performed in Charmides'[18] house near the Olympieum[19] by Alcibiades and Axiochus[20] and Adeimantus.[21] All these fled at that information.

[17] One more information was given. Lydus, belonging to Pherecles of Themacus, gave information that Mysteries were performed in the house of his master Pherecles at Themacus.[22] Among the others that he listed, he said that my father was present but asleep with his face covered. Speusippus, a member of the Council, had them sent for trial, and then my father gave sureties and prosecuted Speusippus for proposing an illegal decree. The trial was held before six thousand Athenians, and from all those jurors Speusippus got less than two hundred votes. And I was the person who most of all begged and

---

[13] The friend of Socrates after whom Plato's *Phaedrus* is named.

[14] A brother of Nicias the general. The third brother, Eucrates, was denounced by Diocleides (1.47).

[15] A different man from Antiphon the orator.

[16] This man is unknown, but his name suggests that he was connected with the aristocratic Alcmeonid family. At least two women in earlier generations of that family (the mother of Cleisthenes and the mother of Pericles) were named Agariste.

[17] This is probably Damon the musician, who had been a friend of Pericles.

[18] This is probably Charmides son of Glaucon, Plato's uncle, who appears in Plato's *Charmides* and Xenophon's *Symposium*.

[19] The temple of Olympian Zeus, southeast of the Acropolis.

[20] Alcibiades' uncle, after whom the dialogue *Axiochus*, attributed to Plato, is named.

[21] A friend of Alcibiades who became a general in the closing years of the Peloponnesian War.

[22] Themacus was a deme (village) in Attica, but its exact location is unknown.

persuaded my father to stay in Athens, and his other relatives did too. [18] Please call Callias[23] and Stephanus. Call Philippus and Alexippus too; they're relatives of Acumenus and Autocrator, who fled because of the information Lydus gave (Autocrator is a nephew of one, and Acumenus an uncle of the other), and it's appropriate for them to feel loathing for the man who banished those two and to know best who caused their exile. Face the jury, and state whether I'm telling the truth.

[WITNESSES]

[19] You've heard the facts, gentlemen, and the witnesses have given you their evidence. But think what the prosecutors were bold enough to say. (This is the right way to defend oneself, by recalling what the prosecutors said and refuting it.) They said that I gave information about the Mysteries, and listed my own father as having been present, and became an informer against my own father—of all things, surely a most dreadful and wicked thing to say! The man who listed him was Pherecles' Lydus, while I was the man who persuaded him to stay in Athens and not flee into exile; I begged him at his knees again and again. [20] But what was my aim, if I informed against my father, as they allege, and yet begged my father to stay and suffer the consequences of my act? And would my father have consented to face a trial like that, in which he couldn't avoid one or other of two disastrous results? Either I should cause his death, if it was decided that my information against him was the truth, or else, if he himself were saved, he would cause my death. For the law was that, if anyone gave true information, he was to have immunity, but if false, he was to be put to death. And of course you all know that my life and my father's were both saved. That couldn't have happened if I'd become an informer against my father; death for either me or him was inevitable. [21] Then again, if my father had wanted to stay in Athens, do you think his friends would have let him stay or have stood surety for him? Wouldn't they have entreated and urged him to go away, so as to save his own life while not causing my death?

[22] Furthermore, when my father was proceeding against Speusippus for his illegal decree, he actually said that he never went to The-

---

macus to see Pherecles, and he urged him to put his slaves to the torture to prove it,[24] and not to refuse to examine people who offered
their slaves for torture while compelling people who refused. When
my father said this, as you all know he did, what could Speusippus say
(if what they say is true) but: "Why do you mention servants, Leogoras? Hasn't your son here informed against you, saying you were
present at Themacus? You, refute your father, or you have no immunity!" Would Speusippus have said that, gentlemen, or not? I think he
would.

[23] If, then, I entered a lawcourt, or anything was said about me,
or there's any information or list of mine, whether given by me against
another man or by someone else against me, anyone who wishes may
come up here and refute me. But in fact I've never known any men
say anything more wicked and more incredible. They thought all they
needed to do was to venture to make an accusation. They didn't care
if they were proved to be lying. [24] Now, if their accusations against
me had been true, I'm the man you'd have been angry with, and you'd
have thought it right to impose the heaviest penalty on me. So, when
you realize they're lying, I say you should consider them criminals
themselves and infer that, if their most serious accusations are clearly
proved to be lies, then it will be easy for me to demonstrate to you
that their far more trivial ones are lies too.

[25] So that's how these four informations about the Mysteries were
given. The names of the men who fled upon each information have
been read to you, and the witnesses have given evidence. Besides this,
I'll do something more to convince you, gentlemen. Some of those
who fled in the case of the Mysteries died in exile, but others have
returned and are in Athens and are present in court at my request.
[26] So I'll give up time from my speech to anyone who wishes to
prove that any of them went into exile because of me, or that I informed against him, or that they didn't each go into exile because of
those informations I described to you. If anyone proves I'm lying, do
what you like with me. I now pause and give way, if anyone wants to
come up.

---

[24] The evidence of slaves was, with certain exceptions, admissible only if given
under torture. See Ant. 1.6n.

[27] Well now, gentlemen, what happened next? After the informations were given, there was a dispute about the rewards—1,000 drachmas according to Cleonymus' decree,[25] 10,000 according to Peisander's[26]—which were claimed by those informants, and by Pythonicus, who said he made the first announcement, and by Androcles on behalf of the Council. [28] So the Assembly resolved that those who had been initiated should decide between the claimants in the court of the Thesmothetae[27] after hearing the information which they'd each given. They voted in favor of Andromachus first and Teucer second, and at the festival of the Panathenaea Andromachus got 10,000 drachmas and Teucer 1,000. Please call the witnesses of this.

[WITNESSES]

[29] As far as the Mysteries are concerned, gentlemen, for which the indictment was brought and which you initiates have come into court to hear about, I've demonstrated that I've neither committed impiety nor informed about anyone nor made a confession about them, nor am I guilty of a single offense, great or small, concerning the Two Goddesses. It's very important for me to convince you of this. For the speeches of the prosecution—they wailed on about those grisly horrors,[28] and they told stories of how other people previously committed offenses and impieties concerning the Two Goddesses, and what punishment each of them suffered. [30] What have those stories and incidents to do with me? On the contrary, I accuse the prosecutors. I say they ought to be put to death for impiety themselves,[29] while I ought to be let off because I've done nothing wrong. It would be shocking

---

[25] The politician Cleonymus is now known to us mainly from Aristophanes' jokes about him as a fat coward.

[26] See 1.36n.

[27] Six of the Archons, whose main responsibility was arranging and presiding over trials.

[28] The awful consequences which the gods would inflict on Athens if those guilty of impiety were not duly punished. One of the stories, concerning a man who was unable to eat and died of starvation, is found in the surviving speech *Against Andocides* (Lys. 6.1).

[29] Andocides means that the prosecutors, when they accuse him of impiety, are guilty of telling lies about a sacred matter.

otherwise, if you condemned me for other men's offenses and, when you know the allegations against me come from my opponents, are going to prefer them to the truth. Obviously people who have committed offenses of this sort can't defend themselves by saying they haven't; trial before men who know the truth is a severe ordeal. But to me proof is a pleasure, since I can secure my acquittal on this serious charge by refuting my opponents' speeches, and I don't need to make any entreaties or appeals to you.

[31] You, whom I'm reminding of the facts, are men who, before casting your votes in my case, have sworn great oaths and invoked the most solemn curses on yourselves and your own children, undertaking to vote for a just verdict on me; and besides you've been initiated and you've seen the sacred rites of the Two Goddesses, so that you may punish the impious and protect the innocent. [32] You must then consider it no less impious to convict the innocent of impiety than to fail to punish those guilty of it. So I call upon you, much more earnestly than my accusers, in the name of the Two Goddesses, for the sake both of the sacred rites which you have seen and of the Greeks who come to Attica for the festival: if I've committed any impiety or confessed it or informed against any human being, or anyone else against me, execute me; I ask no mercy. [33] But if I haven't committed any offense, and if I demonstrate this to you, I ask you to make it clear to the whole of Greece that I didn't deserve to be brought to trial here; for if Cephisius here, my prosecutor, fails to get one-fifth of the votes and is disfranchised,[30] he's not allowed to go into the Two Goddesses' temple, or he'll be put to death.

Now show me if you think I've made an adequate defense on this matter, to encourage me in making the rest of my defense.

[34] As for the mutilation of the images and the information given about it, I'll do just as I promised you: I'll explain all the facts to you from the beginning. When Teucer came from Megara after obtaining immunity, he gave the information he had not only about the Myster-

---

[30] In most public cases a prosecutor who failed to obtain one-fifth of the jury's votes was fined 1,000 drachmas and lost a citizen's right to prosecute in the same type of case in future, on the ground that his prosecution must have been frivolous and unjustified.

ies but also about the mutilators of the images, and he listed eighteen men. When they were listed, some of them fled into exile, while others were arrested and put to death on Teucer's information. Please read their names.

[35] [NAMES] *In the case of the Herms Teucer informed against Euctemon, Glaucippus, Eurymachus, Polyeuctus, Plato,*[31] *Antidorus, Charippus, Theodorus, Alcisthenes, Menestratus, Eryximachus,*[32] *Euphiletus,*[33] *Eurydamas, Pherecles, Meletus,*[34] *Timanthes, Archidamus, Telenicus.*

Now, some of those men have returned and are in Athens, and those who were put to death have left a number of relatives. Any of them who wishes may come up in the time allowed for my speech and refute me by showing that I caused the exile or death of any of those men.

[36] When that happened, Peisander and Charicles, who were members of the commission of inquiry and at that time were thought to be strong supporters of democracy,[35] declared that what had been done was not the work of a few men but was aimed at the overthrow of democracy, and that the search must be continued and not given up. The city was in such a state that, whenever the herald proclaimed that the Council was to go to the Council-house, and took down the signal, at that same signal the Council would go to the Council-house and the people in the Agora would run away, each one terrified of being arrested!

[37] Encouraged by the city's troubles, Diocleides made an announcement to the Council, claiming that he knew the men who mutilated the Herms and that there were about three hundred of them. He said he saw the deed and happened to be there. Please pay close

---

[31] Not the philosopher, nor the comic dramatist of this name.

[32] A doctor, who appears in Plato's *Symposium*.

[33] Andocides' friend; cf. 1.61–64.

[34] See 1.12n.

[35] Four years later, in 411, Peisander certainly and Charicles probably became members of the oligarchic regime of the Four Hundred. Charicles was also a member of the Thirty in 404.

attention, gentlemen, and recollect whether I'm telling the truth, and tell one another about it; for the statements were made in your presence, and you're my witnesses of them.

[38] He said he had a slave at Laurium and had to collect a payment.[36] He got up early, mistaking the time, and started walking; there was a full moon.[37] When he was passing the gateway of Dionysus,[38] he saw a large number of people coming down from the Odeum into the orchestra,[39] and being frightened of them, he went into the shadow and sat down between a pillar and the stone on which the bronze general stands. He saw people, about three hundred in number, standing in groups of fifteen or twenty men, and seeing their faces in the light of the moon he recognized most of them. [39] (He started his story in this way—really a terrible thing to do!—so as to have it in his power to say any Athenian he wished was, or was not, among those men.) After seeing this, he said, he went on to Laurium, and the next day he heard that the Herms had been mutilated. He realized at once that those men were responsible. [40] When he got back to town, he found a commission of inquiry already appointed and a reward of 10,000 drachmas offered for information. Seeing Euphemus, the brother of Callias son of Telocles, sitting in his smithy, he took him up to the temple of Hephaestus[40] and told him what I've told you, that he saw us that night; he'd prefer, he said, to accept money not from the state but from us, so as to be friends with us. Euphemus said he did well to say so and asked him to go now to Leogoras' house, "to meet there, with me, Andocides and some other people you need to see." [41] Diocleides said he did go the next day. He knocked on the door. My father happened to be coming out and said: "Is it you

---

[36] The slave was hired out as a worker in the silver mines at Laurium in southeast Attica.

[37] This detail was supposed to explain how he could see the faces of so many men. But according to Plutarch (*Alcibiades* 20) this was what proved that his story was a lie, because the mutilation of the Herms actually took place on the last night of the month, when there was no moon.

[38] The entrance to the theater of Dionysus, beside the Acropolis.

[39] The chorus's dancing area in the middle of the theater.

[40] The temple still standing on the west side of the Agora, now commonly but wrongly called the Theseum.

they're waiting for? Friends like you certainly mustn't be turned away!"
Having said that, he went off. (In that way he tried to bring about my
father's death, by showing that he was in the know.) We said (he went
on) that we'd decided to offer him two talents[41] of silver, in place of
the 10,000 drachmas from the treasury, and that if we got what we
wanted, he was to be one of us, and that we would exchange pledges
to do all this. [42] His answer to that was that he'd think about it, and
we told him to go to the house of Callias son of Telocles, to enable
him to be present too. (Thus he tried to bring about my brother-in-
law's death.)[42] He said he did go to Callias', and after giving his consent pledged himself to us on the Acropolis; and though we agreed to
pay him the money at the end of the month then beginning, we broke
our word and didn't pay. So now he'd come to give information about
what happened.

[43] Such was Diocleides' statement, gentlemen. He listed the
names of the men he said he'd recognized, forty-two of them: first
Mantitheus and Apsephion, who were members of the Council and
were present at the meeting, and then the rest. Then Peisander stood
up and said the decree of the year of Scamandrius[43] should be repealed
and those listed should be put on to the wheel, to make sure that all the
men were discovered before nightfall. There was a shout of approval
from the Council. [44] When Mantitheus and Apsephion heard this,
they went to sit at the altar,[44] begging not to be tortured but to be
allowed bail and trial. They got this, with some difficulty; and when
they'd provided sureties they mounted their horses and were off, de-
serting to the enemy, leaving behind their sureties, who were to be
liable to the same penalties as the men whose presence they guaranteed. [45] At the end of its meeting the Council's secret decision to
arrest us was carried out. We were put in the stocks in prison. They
called up the generals and told them to proclaim that Athenians living
in town were to go armed to the Agora, those in the Long Walls[45] to

[41] 1 talent = 6,000 drachmas.

[42] Callias son of Telocles had married Andocides' sister.

[43] This decree forbade the torture of Athenian citizens. Its date is not certain,
but may have been 510/09.

[44] To take sanctuary.

[45] The Long Walls ran on either side of the road linking Athens and Piraeus.

the Theseum,[46] and those in Piraeus to the Agora of Hippodamus,[47] and that a trumpet-signal should be given before daybreak for the cavalry to come to the Anaceum,[48] and that the Council was to go to the Acropolis and sleep there, and the Prytaneis in the Tholos.[49] The Boeotians had heard what was going on and were out in force on the frontier.[50] And Diocleides, the man responsible for all this trouble, was being treated as the savior of the city; they were taking him to the Prytaneum in a carriage with a garland on his head, and he was dining there.[51]

[46] So first, gentlemen, those of you who were present should recall what happened and tell the others about it. Then please call the Prytaneis who were in office at that time, Philocrates and the rest. Tell them about it.

[WITNESSES]

[47] Well now, I'll have the names of the men he listed read out to you, to show you how many of my relatives he put at risk of death: first my father and next my brother-in-law, by indicating that the one was in the know and alleging that the meeting took place in the house of the other; and you'll hear the names of the rest. Read out the list for them.

Charmides son of Aristoteles.

That's my cousin. His mother and my father were sister and brother.

Taureas.

---

[46] A temple of Theseus on the north side of the Acropolis.

[47] The town-planner who designed Piraeus.

[48] A temple of the Dioscuri on the north side of the Acropolis.

[49] The Tholos, a round building next to the Council-house in the Agora, was the office of the Prytaneis.

[50] Boeotia was regarded as an enemy of Athens, though war was not actually in progress at this time.

[51] The Prytaneum was another official building on the north side of the Acropolis. Those who had performed special services for Athens were given dinner there.

That's my father's cousin.

Nisaeus.

Taureas' son.

Callias son of Alcmeon.

My father's cousin.

Euphemus.

The brother of Callias son of Telocles.

Phrynichus the former dancer.

A cousin.

Eucrates.

Nicias' brother. He was Callias' brother-in-law.

Critias.[52]

He also was a cousin of my father's; their mothers were sisters. All those were among the forty men he listed.

[48] We were all imprisoned in the same place. Night came on, and the prison was closed up. One man had his mother there, another his sister, another his wife and children, and there were cries and moans from the men as they wept and carried on about the trouble they were in. Then Charmides, my cousin, who was my age and had been brought up with me in our house since we were boys, said to me: [49] "Andocides, you see how serious the situation is. Up till now I didn't want to say anything to annoy you, but now I'm forced to by the trouble we're in. Some of your friends and companions, outside our family, have already been put to death on the same charges that we're facing, and others have gone into exile, condemning themselves as guilty. [50] So if you've heard anything about this business, say so, and save yourself first, and next your father, whom you naturally love

---

[52] This is the Critias who became the leader of the tyrannical regime of the Thirty in 404.

most, and next your brother-in-law, the husband of your only sister, and then all these other relatives and members of the family, and also me. I've never given you any trouble in my whole life, and I've always been ready to support you and your interests."

[51] When Charmides said this, gentlemen, and the rest begged me, and every one of them entreated me, I thought to myself: "I must be the unluckiest man in the world! Am I to do nothing while my own relatives are unjustly destroyed, being put to death and having their property confiscated, and are also recorded on monuments as sinners against the gods, when they're not responsible for any of what has happened? And while three hundred other Athenians are going to be put to death unjustly, and the city is in the greatest trouble and mutual suspicion? Or shall I tell the Athenians what was said to me by Euphiletus, the man who actually did it?" [52] And besides this, gentlemen, I also thought to myself and calculated that some of the guilty men, who did the deed, had already been put to death because of Teucer's information, while others had gone into exile and been condemned to death. But there were four left of those who took part, against whom Teucer didn't inform: Panaetius, Chaeredemus, Diacritus, and Lysistratus. [53] It was reasonable to assume that they above all were among those Diocleides had informed against, since they were friends of the men who were already dead. Their safety was doubtful anyway, while my relatives were obviously going to die if no one made the facts public. So it seemed to me better to deprive four men of their country justly (men who are now alive, and have returned to Athens, and are in possession of their property) than to let my relatives be unjustly put to death.

[54] If any of you other citizens, gentlemen, previously had the idea that I informed against my own comrades to secure their death and my own life (and that's the story my enemies spread about me, to damage my reputation), consider the actual facts. [55] The account I give of my actions now must be truthful, since it's given in the presence of men who actually committed the crime and went into exile because they did it, and who know best whether I'm lying or telling the truth (they can refute me in the time allotted for my speech; I'll permit them). It's important that you should understand what happened, [56] because for me, gentlemen, the essential thing in this trial is that I should be acquitted and have my reputation cleared. It's also

important that everyone else should understand that none of my actions was discreditable or cowardly, but they were all due to the trouble which afflicted the city above all, and also afflicted us, and that my reason for reporting what Euphiletus had said to me was concern for my relatives and family and concern for the city as a whole, and I showed courage, not cowardice, in my opinion. So, if that's the case, I claim I should be acquitted and you should regard me as free from blame.

[57] I ask you, gentlemen, since you ought to reckon cases by human standards, as you would if you were in the trouble yourselves: what would each of you have done? If it had been possible to choose between honorable death and dishonorable survival, my action might be criticized—though a lot of people would have made the same choice even then, preferring life to an honorable death. [58] But where the choice was just the opposite of that, either, if I said nothing, to die myself in the greatest disgrace although I'd committed no impiety, and also to allow the death of my father, my brother-in-law, and all those relatives and cousins, for whose death no one but myself would be responsible if I failed to state that others were guilty (Diocleides, you see, got them imprisoned by his lies, and nothing could save them unless Athens learned the whole story; so I would be their murderer if I didn't report to you what had been said to me)—and I should also be responsible for the death of three hundred Athenians, and the city would be getting into a most serious situation. [59] That's what was going to happen if I said nothing. But if I stated the facts I should be saved myself, and I should save my father and my other relatives, and I should be putting an end to alarm and a most serious situation in Athens. Four men would be exiles because of me; but they were guilty. Of the rest, against whom Teucer informed earlier, the dead were surely not going to be any more dead because of me, nor the exiles more exiled. [60] Considering all this, gentlemen, I found that the least of the evils was to state the facts at once, and to prove that Diocleides had been lying and get him punished. He was causing us to be put to death unjustly, and he was deceiving Athens, and for doing so he was being regarded as a hero and was getting a reward.

[61] For these reasons I told the Council that I knew who had done it, and I revealed the facts. I said that Euphiletus suggested the plan while we were having a drink, and I spoke against it, and on that

occasion I was responsible for the plan's rejection. But later, while riding at Cynosarges[53] on a pony of mine, I had a fall, and I broke my collar-bone and cut my head, and was carried home on a stretcher. [62] When Euphiletus saw how I was, he said to them that I'd been persuaded to join in and had told him I agreed to take part and to mutilate the Herm near the shrine of Phorbas. But when he told them this, he was lying; and that's why the Herm you can all see, the one near our family home, set up by the Aegeis tribe,[54] was the only Herm in Athens not mutilated—because they thought I was going to do it, as Euphiletus had told them. [63] When they realized, they made quite a fuss because I knew about the business but hadn't taken part. Next day Meletus and Euphiletus came to me and said: "We've done it, Andocides, and carried it out. As for you, if you're willing to keep quiet and say nothing, we'll be your friends as before. But if not, you'll suffer more from our enmity than you'll gain from any friends you acquire by what you say about us." [64] I told them I thought it was criminal of Euphiletus to do it, but that I was no danger to them because I knew about it; a far greater danger was the crime itself, just because it had been committed.

To show that this was true, I handed over my slave for torture to prove that I'd been ill and hadn't even been getting up from my bed; and the maidservants of the house which they used as their base were seized by the Prytaneis. [65] The Council and the commission of inquiry examined the matter; and since it was as I said, and it was universally agreed, they then summoned Diocleides. Not many words were needed, but he immediately admitted he'd been lying, and asked to be let off if he stated who were the men who persuaded him to tell his story. They were Alcibiades of Phegus[55] and Amiantus from Aegina. [66] Those men were terrified and fled into exile. When you heard this, you handed Diocleides over to a lawcourt and executed him. You released my relatives who were in prison and were going to be put to death because of me, and you let those in exile return. You

---

[53] A place to the east of the town, with a shrine of Heracles and a gymnasium.

[54] One of the ten tribes in which Athenian citizens were organized, named after the legendary king Aegeus.

[55] Not to be confused with the famous Alcibiades.

yourselves went home with your weapons, freed from a great deal of trouble and danger.

[67] In all this, gentlemen, I deserve everyone's sympathy for what happened to me, and I can reasonably be praised for what I did. When Euphiletus suggested one of the most treacherous pledges[56] that men could make, I opposed him, spoke against him, and scolded him as he deserved. After they committed the crime I helped them to conceal it, and it was because Teucer informed against them that some were executed and others went into exile; that was before we were imprisoned by Diocleides and were going to be put to death. Then I did list four men, Panaetius, Diacritus, Lysistratus, and Chaeredemus. [68] They went into exile because of me, I admit. But my father was saved, and my brother-in-law, three cousins, and seven other relatives,[57] who were going to be executed unjustly. They owe it to me that they now see the light of day, and they themselves admit it. And the man who threw the whole city into confusion and brought it into the utmost danger was shown up, and you were freed from great alarm and mutual suspicion.

[69] Recollect, gentlemen, whether what I say is true; and those of you who saw it, explain it to the others. And you, please call the actual men who were released because of me. They best know the facts and can tell the jury about them. It's like this, men of the jury: they'll come up and speak to you for as long as you want to listen to them, and after that I'll make my defense on the rest of the case.

[WITNESSES]

[70] Now you've heard everything, and I've completed my defense about what happened at that time—at least I believe so, but if any of you wants anything more or thinks some point hasn't been explained adequately, or if I've left something out, he has only to stand up and mention it, and I'll make my defense to that too. Now I'll explain to you about the laws.

---

[56] The mutilation of the Herms was a pledge, in the sense that mutual knowledge of their guilt would guarantee the conspirators' loyalty to one another.

[57] These numbers do not fit the list in 1.47, and there may be some error in the text.

[71] Cephisius here used the existing law to prosecute me, but in presenting his case he's using an earlier decree proposed by Isotimides, which has nothing to do with me. Isotimides proposed that those who had committed impiety and had confessed it should be excluded from the holy places. But I haven't done either of those things; I've neither committed impiety nor confessed it. [72] Besides, that decree has been annulled and is invalid, as I'll explain to you. But the peculiar thing about this defense is that, whereas I shall be punished myself if I don't convince you, if I do convince you I shall have made a defense for my opponents.[58] Still, the truth shall be told.

[73] After the navy was destroyed and the siege began,[59] you had a discussion about unity. You decided to enfranchise the disfranchised, and Patrocleides proposed his decree. Who were the disfranchised, and what rights had each of them lost? I'll explain to you. Some owed money to the treasury; they were men who had been found guilty at the examination after they held office, or who had been found guilty of failing to pay a legal debt or of public offenses, or who owed fines, or who had purchased tax-collecting rights from the treasury and failed to pay the money, or who had acted as sureties to the treasury (these had to pay during the ninth Prytany;[60] otherwise they had to pay double, and their property was confiscated for sale). [74] Also any men who had been found guilty of embezzlement or corruption; these men's descendants, as well as themselves, had to be disfranchised.[61] That was one type of disfranchisement. Another was of those who themselves were disfranchised, but kept possession of their property. These were men guilty of desertion or evasion of military service or cowardice or evasion of naval service or throwing away their shields,[62]

---

[58] Andocides means that, if the amnesty is not regarded as valid, three of his prosecutors will themselves be liable to prosecution, as explained in 1.92–100.

[59] In 405.

[60] A Prytany was the period of office of one group of Prytaneis. There were ten Prytanies in the year, each lasting 36 or 37 days.

[61] The position of this sentence in the text is problematical. The manuscript has it a few lines later, after ". . . kept possession of their property." Reasons for the transposition to the beginning of 74 are given in *Revue Internationale des Droits de l'Antiquité* 30 (1983): 69–76.

[62] Throwing away his shield was the characteristic act of a man running away in a battle.

or who had been found guilty of giving false evidence on three occasions or falsely testifying to a summons on three occasions, or who had maltreated their parents. All these were themselves disfranchised but kept their money. [75] Others again were disfranchised in specified ways; they were not disfranchised entirely, but in some part. For example, the soldiers who remained in Athens in the time of the tyrants [63] had all the same rights as the other citizens except that they weren't allowed to speak in the Assembly or be members of the Council. Those were the rights they lost, as specified in each case. [76] Others were forbidden to bring a public prosecution (*graphē*), and others to bring an indictment (*endeixis*).[64] Some were forbidden specifically to travel to the Hellespont, others to Ionia, and some to enter the Agora. You voted that all these decrees should be abolished, both the documents themselves and any copy that existed anywhere, and that pledges for unity should be exchanged on the Acropolis. Please read the decree of Patrocleides, by which this was done.

[77] [DECREE] *Patrocleides proposed: Since the Athenians voted that it should be permitted to make proposals concerning disfranchised persons and public debtors and put them to the vote, the people are to vote the same decree as during the Persian Wars, when it was beneficial to Athens. Concerning those registered with the Practores[65] or with the treasurers of the Goddess and of the other gods or with the Basileus,[66] or anyone whose name was not written down, up to the end of the term of office of the Council when Callias was Archon,[67] [78] all disfranchised persons and public debtors, and all who have been declared guilty of misconduct in office by the examiners and their assessors in the auditors' offices, or who face prosecutions which have not yet come into court concerning the examination of their conduct in office, or who have been condemned to suffer specific restrictions or to forfeit securities, up to the same date, and all the names of any of the Four Hundred that are registered, or any other record anywhere of what was done*

---

[63] Here "the tyrants" means the oligarchic regime of the Four Hundred in 411.

[64] See 1.33n.

[65] The Practores were revenue-collecting officials.

[66] The Basileus was one of the nine Archons, with responsibility especially for religious matters.

[67] Callias of Angele was chief Archon in 406/5.

during the oligarchy—except for all names, inscribed on stone, of those
who did not remain in Athens[68] *or who, having been tried by either*
the Areopagus or the Ephetae or at the Prytaneum or the Delphinium
under the presidency of the Basileis,[69] *are in some exile for homicide or*
were condemned to death as murderers or tyrants— [79] *all the other*
names mentioned shall be obliterated by the Practores and the Coun-
cil from every place where any of them is recorded in public, and the
Thesmothetae and other officials shall produce any copy that exists any-
where. This is to be done within three days after the people's resolution.
It shall not be permitted for anyone to keep a private record of the
names whose obliteration has been ordered, nor ever to revive accusa-
tions; otherwise the transgressor of this rule shall be liable to the same
penalties as those exiled by the Areopagus, so that there may be as much
mutual trust as possible in Athens both now and in the future.

[80] By this decree you enfranchised the disfranchised. But Patrocleides didn't propose, and you didn't vote, that exiles should return.
After the truce was made with the Spartans, and you demolished the
walls, and you accepted the return of exiles, and the Thirty were established, and then Phyle was seized, and they seized Munychia, you
had experiences which I needn't recall, nor need I remind you of the
troubles which followed.[70] [81] After your return to Athens from Piraeus,[71] though it was in your power to take revenge, you decided to
let bygones be bygones. You thought the preservation of Athens more
important than personal vengeance, and you resolved not to revive accusations against one another for what had happened. On this resolution you appointed twenty men; they were to have charge of the city
until fresh laws were made. Meanwhile the laws of Solon and the ordinances of Draco were to be employed.[72] [82] After you had drawn

---

[68] The oligarchic leaders who fled into exile to avoid execution.

[69] The courts which tried cases of homicide.

[70] This sentence summarizes the events of 404/3. The prodemocratic party,
opposing the Thirty, occupied Phyle in northern Attica and then Munychia near
Piraeus.

[71] Andocides assumes that all his listeners were with the Thirty's opponents,
who used Piraeus as their base in the civil war which led to the restoration of
democracy in 403.

[72] These were the traditional laws of Athens, reputedly introduced by Draco
in the late seventh century and Solon in the early sixth.

lots for a Council and appointed lawmakers, they found that under
many of the laws of Solon and Draco many citizens were liable to penalties for what they'd done earlier. You called an Assembly, discussed
them, and voted that all the laws should be examined, and then those
laws which were approved should be inscribed in the Stoa.[73] Please
read the decree.

[83] [DECREE] *The people resolved, Teisamenus proposed: The Athenians shall conduct their public affairs in the traditional manner.
They shall employ the laws of Solon and his weights and measures, and
they shall employ also the ordinances of Draco, which we employed in
former times. Such additions as are needed shall be inscribed on boards
by the lawmakers appointed by the Council, and shall be exhibited in
front of the tribal heroes[74] for all to see and handed over to the officials
within this month.* [84] *The laws which are handed over shall be examined first by the Council and by the five hundred lawmakers appointed by the members of the demes, after they have taken the oath.
Also any individual who wishes shall be permitted to come before the
Council and make any good suggestion he can about the laws. After
the laws are passed, the council of the Areopagus shall take care of the
laws, to ensure that officials employ the laws which are in force. Those
laws which are ratified shall be inscribed on the wall, where they were
inscribed before, for anyone who wishes to read them.*

[85] So the laws were examined in accordance with this decree, and
the ones which were ratified were inscribed in the Stoa. When they'd
been inscribed, we passed a law which is universally enforced. Please
read the law.

[LAW] *A law which has not been inscribed shall not be employed by
officials on any matter whatever.*

[86] Is there thus anything left about which an official could bring
a case to court or any of you could take action, except in accordance
with the inscribed laws? Well then, where an uninscribed law may not
be employed, still more must an uninscribed decree not be enforced
at all. So, since we saw that a number of citizens were in trouble, some
with laws and some with decrees previously passed, we passed these

---

[73] Laws were inscribed on the walls of the Stoa Basileios in the Agora.

[74] The statues of the ten heroes after whom the Athenian tribes were named.

laws with a view to exactly what is now going on, so that none of this might happen and no one might be allowed to prosecute anyone maliciously. Please read the laws.

[87] [LAWS] *A law which has not been inscribed shall not be employed by officials on any matter whatever.*

No decree of the Council or Assembly shall prevail over a law.

It shall not be permitted to pass a law applying to an individual unless the same law applies to all Athenians, unless it is resolved by six thousand voting by secret ballot.

What else was there? This law. Please read this one.

[LAW] *All judgments and arbitrations shall be valid which were given while the city was democratically governed. The laws shall be applied from the Archonship of Eucleides.*[75]

[88] So, gentlemen, you made all judgments and arbitrations valid which were given while the city was democratically governed, so that debts might not be canceled nor cases retried, but agreements between individuals might be carried out.[76] For offenses dealt with by public prosecution (*graphē*) or denunciation (*phasis*) or indictment (*endeixis*) or arrest (*apagōgē*)[77] you voted that the laws should be applied from the archonship of Eucleides. [89] So, when you had resolved that the laws should be examined, and that after being approved they should be inscribed, and that a law which had not been inscribed should not be employed by officials on any matter whatever, and that no decree of the Council or Assembly should prevail over a law, and that a law applying to an individual should not be passed unless the same law applied to all Athenians, and that the laws in force should be applied from the Archonship of Eucleides, is there anything left here, great or small, of the decrees which were passed before Eucleides became Archon, which will be valid? I think not, gentlemen. Consider it for yourselves.

---

[75] Eucleides was chief Archon in 403/2.

[76] The decree of Patrocleides had invalidated judgments in many public cases tried before 405, including debts owed to public funds. The law just quoted confirmed the validity of judgments in private cases already tried, including debts owed to individuals.

[77] These are all procedures used for prosecution in public cases.

[90] And now, how do your oaths go? There's the one the whole city shared, which you all swore after the reconciliations: "And I will not revive accusations against any citizen except the Thirty and the Eleven,[78] nor against any of them who are willing to undergo examination of their conduct in office." When you swore not to revive accusations even against the Thirty, who were the greatest criminals, if they underwent examination, you can hardly have thought it right to revive accusations against any of the other citizens. [91] Again, what is sworn by the Council holding office each year? "And I will not accept any indictment or arrest for what happened earlier, except against those who fled into exile." Again, what do you swear, Athenians, before sitting as jurors? "And I will not revive accusations nor accept those revived by anyone else, but I will vote in accordance with the laws in force." You must consider these facts, to see whether you think I'm right when I tell you that I'm speaking in support of yourselves and the laws.

[92] Now, gentlemen, consider together the laws and the prosecutors, to see what their own position is while they're accusing other people. Cephisius here purchased a tax-collecting right from the treasury, and after collecting the proceeds of this from the farmers of the land concerned, which amounted to 9,000 drachmas, he didn't pay up to the city; and he fled into exile, because if he'd come to Athens he'd have been imprisoned in the stocks. [93] The law went like this: "The Council shall have authority to imprison in the stocks any purchaser of a tax who does not pay up." Now, because you voted that the laws should be applied from the Archonship of Eucleides, this man thinks it right not to pay over your money that he's collected. He's now been transformed from an exile into a citizen, and from a disfranchised man into a malicious accuser, because you apply the laws now in force.

[94] Again, Meletus here arrested Leon in the time of the Thirty,[79]

---

[78] The Eleven were officials in charge of the prison, responsible for arrests and executions.

[79] The Thirty ordered five men to arrest Leon of Salamis. Socrates, as well as Meletus, was among the five, but he refused to carry out the order (see Plato, *Apology* 32c–d). One of the prosecutors of Socrates in 399 was also named Meletus, but he was a young man previously unknown to Socrates (see Plato, *Euthyphro* 2b) and so is unlikely to have been the same person.

as you all know, and Leon was executed without trial. And the following law not only existed in the past but also exists and is applied even
now, because it's a good one: "One who has planned an act shall be
liable to the same penalty as one who has committed it with his own
hand." So the reason why Leon's sons aren't allowed to prosecute Meletus for murder is that the laws have to be applied from the Archonship of Eucleides; for not even the man himself denies that he made
the arrest.

[95] Epichares here, an utter scoundrel and pleased to be one, who
revives accusations against himself—! He was a member of the Council in the time of the Thirty: but what does the law say, the one inscribed on stone in front of the Council-house? "Anyone who holds
office in the city when the democracy has been subverted may be
killed with impunity, and the killer shall be free from guilt and shall
possess the dead man's property." So isn't it the case, Epichares, that
anyone who kills you now will have untainted hands, according to
Solon's law?[80] [96] Please read the law from the stone.

> [LAW] *It was resolved by the Council and the Assembly; the Aiantis*
> *tribe were Prytaneis; Cleigenes was secretary; Boethus was chairman;*
> *Demophantus drew up the following proposal. This decree dates from*
> *the Council of five hundred appointed by lot for whom Cleigenes was*
> *the first secretary.*
>
> *If anyone subverts the democracy at Athens or holds any office when*
> *the democracy has been subverted, he shall be regarded as an enemy of*
> *the Athenians and may be killed with impunity, and his property shall*
> *be confiscated and a tenth part of it devoted to the Goddess; and he*
> *who kills or helps to plan the killing of anyone who does that shall be*
> *pure and free from guilt.* [97] *All Athenians shall swear over unblem-*
> *ished sacrifices by tribes and by demes to kill anyone who does that.*
> *The oath shall be as follows: "I shall kill, by word and deed, by vote*
> *and by my own hand, if I can, anyone who subverts the democracy at*
> *Athens, and anyone who holds any office after the democracy has been*
> *subverted, and anyone who sets himself up to be tyrant or helps to set*
> *up the tyrant. If anyone else kills him, I shall consider that man to be*

---

[80] Andocides calls it "Solon's law" because it is one of the established laws of
Athens, even though the prescript of the law itself shows that it was passed in 410.

pure in the sight of gods and divinities, because he has killed an enemy
of the Athenians, and I will sell all the property of the dead man and
give half to the killer and not keep any back. [98] *If anyone dies while*
killing or attempting to kill any such man, I will care both for him
and for his children, just as for Harmodius and Aristogeiton and their
descendants.[81] *All oaths that have been sworn against the people of*
Athens, at Athens or on campaign or anywhere else, I declare null and
void." All Athenians shall swear this oath over unblemished sacrifices
in the customary manner before the Dionysia,[82] *and they shall pray*
that he who keeps his oath may have many blessings, but that he who
breaks it may suffer destruction, both himself and his family.

[99] Tell me, you malicious accuser, you damned fox, is this law
valid or not valid? The reason why it's become invalid, surely, is that
the laws have to be applied from the Archonship of Eucleides. And so
you are alive, and walk around this city, though you don't deserve it.
Under the democracy you lived by accusing, and under the oligarchy,
to avoid being forced to pay back the money you got by accusing, you
groveled to the Thirty. [100] And then do you talk to me about friends
and find fault with people? You were not just one man's boy-friend
(you'd have been okay then); you let anyone pay you a small sum, as
the jury knows, and made a living by vice in spite of your ugly looks.
Yet this man dared to accuse other people, when by the laws of Athens
he can't even defend himself!

[101] As I sat here while he was speaking for the prosecution, gentlemen, and as I looked at him, it seemed just as if I'd been arrested
and put on trial by the Thirty. If I'd been in court then, who'd be
accusing me? Wasn't Epichares there to do it, if I didn't buy him off?
So he is now. And who'd be doing the questioning but Charicles?[83]
"Tell me, Andocides," he'd ask, "did you go to Deceleia[84] and for-

---

[81] Harmodius and Aristogeiton in 514 assassinated Hipparchus, brother of the
tyrant Hippias, and they and their descendants were honored as tyrannicides ever
afterwards.

[82] The festival of Dionysus, held in the spring of each year.

[83] See 1.36n.

[84] Deceleia in Attica was captured and fortified by the Spartans as a base for
operations against Athens in the latter part of the Peloponnesian War, and they

tify it against your country?" "No, I didn't." "Well, did you plunder the countryside, and rob your fellow-citizens by land or sea?" "No." "Didn't you even fight against Athens at sea, or help to demolish the walls, or help to subvert the democracy, or force your way back to Athens?" "No, I haven't done any of those things." "None at all? Then do you expect to get away without being put to death, as a lot of other people have been?" [102] Do you think I'd have got any other treatment than that, because of my loyalty to you, gentlemen, if they'd caught me? Then won't it be shocking if, although they would have put me to death like other people because I committed no offense against Athens, I'm not acquitted by you when I've done you no harm? Surely I will be; hardly anyone else will be, otherwise.

[103] Although, gentlemen, they used a law now in force to bring the indictment against me, in presenting the case they used the decree made earlier about other people. If you convict me, consider that it may be more appropriate for a lot of other citizens to give an account of their actions than it is for me: first, the men you fought against, with whom you swore oaths of reconciliation; second, the men you allowed to return from exile; third, the disfranchised men whom you enfranchised. For their sake you removed inscribed stones, you repealed laws, and you abolished decrees; and now they're residing in Athens, relying on your support, gentlemen. [104] If they see you're accepting prosecutions for past acts, what do you suppose they'll think of their own position? Which of them do you think will be willing to face a trial for his past acts? Plenty of opponents and plenty of malicious accusers will appear, to bring every one of them to trial. [105] Both are now here in court to listen, but for different purposes. Some want to know whether they should rely on the laws now in force and on your mutual oaths. The others are gauging your intentions, to see whether they'll be allowed with impunity to make malicious accusations, by public prosecution (*graphē*) and by indictment (*endeixis*) and by arrest (*apagōgē*). This is how it is, gentlemen: it's my life which is at stake in this trial, but the public in general will learn from your

---

were joined there by leading members of the oligarchy of Four Hundred when that regime was overthrown in 411. Andocides implies that Charicles himself participated in this and in the other traitorous acts mentioned in the questions that follow.

vote whether they should rely on the laws of Athens, or bribe the accusers, or leave Athens and get away from them as fast as possible.

[106] To show you, gentlemen, that the action you've taken to
achieve unity isn't misguided, but appropriate and beneficial to yourselves, I want to say a few words about this too. Your ancestors, at a
time when Athens was in a very serious situation, while the tyrants
controlled the city and the democrats were in exile, defeated the tyrants in battle at Pallenion.[85] Among the generals were Leogoras, my
great-grandfather, and Charias, the father of his wife, who was the
mother of my grandfather. On their return to their own country your
ancestors put some to death and condemned some to exile, and others
they allowed to stay in Athens but disfranchised. [107] Later, when the
King of Persia invaded Greece, realizing the immensity of the disaster
which threatened them and the extent of the King's forces, they decided to allow the exiles to return, to enfranchise the disfranchised,
and to share safety and dangers alike. After doing this and exchanging
pledges and solemn oaths, they ventured to put themselves in the front
line, before the whole of Greece, and face the barbarians at Marathon, believing that their own courage was sufficient to set against the
large numbers of the enemy. They fought, and they won. They freed
Greece, and they saved their own country. [108] And after this great
achievement they decided not to revive accusations against anyone for
past acts. It was for this very reason that, finding their city in ruins,
temples burned down, and walls and houses demolished, and starting
from scratch, because of their unity with one another they were able
to establish their Greek empire and hand down to you this fine, great
city.[86] [109] Later you yourselves, in the face of hardship no less than
theirs, were as good as your fathers and showed the generous spirit
that was in you: you decided to allow the exiles to return and to en-

---

[85] Andocides may be confused about the historical details. The battle of Pal-
lene, if that is what he means, was won, not lost, by the tyrant Peisistratus about
546; but he seems to be thinking of a battle in 510, when the descendants of
Peisistratus were expelled.

[86] Andocides has combined the two Persian invasions of Greece, in 490 and
480–479. The battle of Marathon was won by Athens in 490. The city of Athens
was destroyed in 480; its rebuilding and the establishment of the Athenian Empire
took place in the years following the repulse of the Persians in 479.

franchise the disfranchised.[87] So what do you still have to do to equal your ancestors' generosity? Not to revive accusations, gentlemen, remembering that in the old days Athens, starting from far smaller foundations, became great and prosperous. And she can do the same now, if we citizens would only act sensibly and live in unity with one another.

[110] They also accused me about the suppliant-branch.[88] They said I placed it in the Eleusinium,[89] but there was a traditional law that anyone who placed a suppliant-branch at the time of the Mysteries should die. And they're so brazen that, when they themselves contrived the offense, it's not enough for them that their plot failed, but they actually accuse me of committing it! [111] When we returned from Eleusis[90] and the indictment had been brought, the Basileus came to report on the performance of the ritual at Eleusis, as is the custom. The Prytaneis said they would bring him before the Council, and they told him to give notice to Cephisius and me to be present at the Eleusinium. (The Council was to sit there in accordance with Solon's law, which says it is to hold a session in the Eleusinium on the day after the Mysteries.) [112] We were there, as instructed. When the Council was full, Callias son of Hipponicus, wearing his official dress, stood up and said that a suppliant-branch was lying on the altar, and he pointed it out to them. Then the herald made a proclamation asking who placed the suppliant-branch, and no one answered. We were standing by, and this man[91] could see us. When no one answered, and Eucles here[92] had gone inside after making the inquiry—and please call him. First give evidence whether I've been telling the truth, Eucles.

---

[87] In 405 and 404, as explained earlier in the speech.

[88] If Andocides had placed an olive-branch on an altar as a suppliant, that would have implied that he was imploring the gods' forgiveness, and thus that he admitted he was guilty of an offense against them.

[89] The temple in Athens of the Two Goddesses of Eleusis, Demeter and her daughter.

[90] At the end of the annual celebration of the Mysteries at Eleusis.

[91] Cephisius, who was also waiting outside the Eleusinium. Andocides implies that Cephisius had not yet been told by Callias that Andocides was to be accused of placing the suppliant-branch, and therefore did not point him out to the herald.

[92] Eucles was the herald of the Council and the Assembly.

[WITNESS]

[113] Evidence has been given that I'm telling the truth, and I think it's quite different from what the prosecution said. They asserted, if you remember, that the Two Goddesses themselves dazed me so that I placed the suppliant-branch in ignorance of the law, in order that I might be punished. My reply, gentlemen, is that, even if the prosecution's statement is absolutely true, it was the Two Goddesses themselves who saved me. [114] For if I placed the suppliant-branch there and then failed to answer the herald, wasn't I causing my own death by placing the branch, and wasn't it chance that saved me because I failed to answer, for which the Two Goddesses were obviously responsible? If the Goddesses had wanted to kill me, surely I should have admitted placing the branch even if I hadn't done so. But I didn't answer, and I didn't place it.

[115] When Eucles told the Council that no one answered, Callias stood up again and said there was a traditional law that anyone who placed a suppliant-branch in the Eleusinium should be put to death without trial, and his father Hipponicus had once expounded this to the Athenians, and that he'd been told that I was the person who'd placed the branch. Then Cephalus here [93] jumped up and said: [116] "I never heard such blasphemy, Callias! In the first place, you're expounding religious law, but you, as a member of the Ceryces, have no right to expound it. [94] And next, you talk about a traditional law, but the inscribed stone just beside you says that anyone who places a suppliant-branch in the Eleusinium is to be fined 1,000 drachmas. And next, who told you Andocides placed the branch? Call him before the Council, so that he can tell us too." When the inscription was read out, and Callias couldn't say who told him, it was obvious to the Council that he'd placed the branch himself.

[117] And now, gentlemen, perhaps you'd like to hear what Callias

---

[93] Cephalus was a supporter of Andocides at this trial (1.150). He became a prominent politician in subsequent years.

[94] The two aristocratic families of the Eumolpidae and the Ceryces had charge of the Eleusinian Mysteries, but only the former had the right to expound religious law.

was aiming at when he placed the branch. I'll explain to you why he devised his plot against me.

Epilycus son of Teisander was my uncle, my mother's brother.[95] When he died in Sicily, he had no sons, but he left two daughters, who were to pass to Leagrus and me.[96] [118] His financial affairs were in a bad way: he left visible property amounting to less than 2 talents, but his debts were over 5 talents. Still, I invited Leagrus to meet me in the presence of the family, and said that in that sort of situation the decent thing to do was to behave like relatives. [119] "It's not right for us to prefer another estate or a successful man and look down on Epilycus' daughters. After all, if Epilycus were alive, or had left a large amount of money when he died, we should expect to have the girls because we're the nearest relatives. So whereas in that case we should have done so because of Epilycus or because of his money, as things are we'll do it because we're good men. You put in a claim for one, and I will for the other." [120] He agreed with me, gentlemen, and we both put in claims in accordance with our agreement. The girl I claimed happened to fall ill and die, but the other is still living. Callias tried to persuade Leagrus to let him take this girl, and promised him money. When I saw what was going on, I straightaway put down the court fee and got leave to make a claim, first of all saying to Leagrus: "If you want to continue your claim, keep her, and the best of luck! But otherwise I'll put in a claim." [121] When Callias realized this, he got leave to claim the heiress for his own son,[97] on the 10th of the month; and to prevent me from making a claim, after the 20th, at the time of the recent Mysteries, he paid Cephisius 1,000 drachmas to bring an indictment against me and involve me in this trial. After he saw I was staying to face it, he placed the suppliant-branch. His aim was to get me executed without trial or drive me into exile, and to live

---

[95] Epilycus had been an Athenian delegate negotiating with the King of Persia; see 3.29.

[96] Andocides and Leagrus, nephews of Epilycus, were his nearest surviving male relatives, and thus were entitled to claim his daughters in marriage, along with his property.

[97] Callias' son was a more distant relative of Epilycus, but the exact relationship is uncertain.

with Epilycus' daughter himself, by bribing Leagrus. [122] But when he saw that even then he wasn't going to get his way without a trial, he finally went to Lysistratus, Hegemon, and Epichares,[98] seeing that they were close friends of mine, and did something quite disgusting and illegal: he told them that if I was willing to give up Epilycus' daughter even now, he was ready to stop attacking me, call off Cephisius, and pay me compensation agreed by the family for what he'd done. [123] I told him to go ahead, both with the prosecution and with procuring other men to help him. "If I escape him," I said, "and the Athenians give a just verdict in my case, I think it will be his turn to find himself in danger." And if you so decide, gentlemen, I won't disappoint him in this. Please call the witnesses to confirm my statements.

[WITNESSES]

[124] But let me tell you how this son of his, for whom he wanted to claim Epilycus' daughter, was born, and how he acknowledged him. It's certainly worth hearing, gentlemen. Callias married a daughter of Ischomachus;[99] and after living with her for less than a year he took her mother,[100] and the utter scoundrel went on living with the mother and the daughter (though he's a priest of the Mother and the Daughter!)[101] and kept them both in his house. [125] He wasn't ashamed of himself, and showed no fear of the Two Goddesses. But Ischomachus' daughter thought it would be better to die than to live seeing what was going on. She tried to hang herself, but before she'd finished she was taken down and put to bed. After she recovered, she ran away from the house; and so the mother ousted the daughter. Later, when he'd had enough of her, he turned her out too. She said

---

[98] Evidently a different Epichares from the one supporting the prosecution (1.95).

[99] This Ischomachus may be the wealthy man who appears in Xenophon's *Oeconomicus*.

[100] Her name was Chrysilla (1.127). It is possible but not certain that she was the woman who appears in Xenophon as Ischomachus' very young wife. By the time of the present speech Ischomachus must have died, or have divorced her.

[101] The Two Goddesses, Demeter and her daughter.

she was pregnant by him, but when she gave birth to a son he denied that the baby was his. [126] The woman's relatives took the baby and came to the altar at the festival of the Apaturia[102] bringing an animal for sacrifice, and told Callias to begin the ceremony. He asked who was the baby's father. They answered "Callias son of Hipponicus." "That's me!" "Yes, and it's your baby." He put his hand on the altar and solemnly swore that he had no other son, and had never had, but Hipponicus by the daughter of Glaucon, or if he lied he and his family should be utterly destroyed—as they will be!

[127] Some time after this, gentlemen, he fell in love with the old battle-ax again and brought her back into his house, and he introduced the boy, who was quite big by now, into the Ceryces, asserting that he was his own son. Callicles[103] spoke against his acceptance, but the Ceryces voted, in accordance with their law, that the father should introduce him after swearing solemnly that he was introducing his own son. He put his hand on the altar and solemnly swore that the boy was his own legitimate son by Chrysilla—the boy he previously disowned on oath! Please call the witnesses to all this.

[WITNESSES]

[128] And now, gentlemen, let's consider whether such a thing ever happened in Greece before. A man married a wife, and then married the mother after the daughter, and the mother ousted the daughter; and while living with her he wants to have Epilycus' daughter, so that the granddaughter may oust the grandmother.[104] What ought we to call his son? [129] I shouldn't think anyone is good enough at calculating to work out what to call him. There are three women with whom his father will have lived, and he's the son of one (so he says), the

---

[102] The annual festival of phratries (clans) and aristocratic families, at which babies were formally received into them. Callias himself was the presiding priest of his family, the Ceryces.

[103] This reading is a conjectural emendation. The manuscript gives the name as Callides, but no Athenian of that name is known in this period. If Callicles is right, this is the Callicles who appears in Plato's *Gorgias*; he was put to death by the Thirty in 404/3 (Lys. 30.14, where likewise I emend Calliades to Callicles).

[104] Epilycus' wife was a daughter of Chrysilla and (presumably) Ischomachus, so that Chrysilla was the grandmother of Epilycus' daughter.

brother of another, and the uncle of the third. Who can he be? Oedipus? Aegisthus?[105] Or what name should we give him?

[130] But I want to remind you, gentlemen, of a small matter connected with Callias. If you remember, at the time when Athens ruled Greece and was at the height of her success, and Hipponicus[106] was the richest man in Greece, you all know that tiny children and silly women all through the city used to tell a tale that Hipponicus kept a devil in his house, who upturned his table.[107] You remember that, men of the jury. [131] Now how do you think that old story has turned out? When Hipponicus thought he was keeping a son, he was really keeping a devil for himself, who has upturned his riches, his frugality, and all the rest of his way of life. That's how you ought to think of Callias, as Hipponicus' devil.

[132] But, gentlemen, these men who are now supporting Callias in his attack on me, and helped him to procure the trial, and contributed money to deal with me—why is it that I've been in Athens for three years since my return from Cyprus without their thinking me guilty of impiety? I've initiated A . . .[108] the Delphian and other friends of mine, and I've entered the Eleusinium and made sacrifices, as I believe I have a right to do. But so far from thinking me impious, they proposed me for liturgies,[109] first as Gymnasiarch at the Hephaestia,[110] then as Architheorus at the Isthmus and at Olympia.[111] I was also a

---

[105] In myth Oedipus married his mother, Jocasta, without knowing who she was, and Aegisthus was the son of Thyestes and his daughter Pelopeia. Neither of these cases is really parallel to that of Callias' son; Andocides is being sarcastic.

[106] Callias' father.

[107] In Greek this is a pun, because the word for "table" (*trapeza*) is also the word for "bank."

[108] The rest of the name of the man whom Andocides introduced to the Mysteries is lost.

[109] Liturgies were expensive public services which wealthy men were called on to provide. These included service as a trierarch (sponsor of a trireme) or as a choregus (sponsor of a choral performance; cf. Ant. 6), as well as the less important positions mentioned in this sentence.

[110] A Gymnasiarch sponsored the runners for a torch-race, in this case at the festival of Hephaestus.

[111] An Architheorus sponsored the Athenian representatives at one of the great

treasurer of the sacred money on the Acropolis. And now I'm guilty of impiety, am I, and commit an offense by entering the holy places?

[133] I'll tell you why they now take this view. This very respectable gentleman Agyrrhius[112] was chairman of the purchasers of the 2 percent tax[113] two years ago. He bought it for 30 talents. He shared it with all those men who foregathered with him under the poplar;[114] you know what sort of men they are! I suppose the reason why they gathered there was to get two things: to be paid for not outbidding him, and to get shares in the tax-collection when it had been sold at a low price. [134] They made a profit of 3 talents, and when they realized what the business was like, how valuable it was, they all combined, gave shares to the other bidders, and tried to buy it for 30 talents again. Since no one was competing with them, I myself went to the Council and kept outbidding them, until I bought it for 36 talents. Having ousted them, I provided sureties for the state, and then collected the money and paid it over. I didn't lose by it either, but my partners and I actually managed to make a small profit; and I prevented my opponents from distributing among themselves 6 talents of your money.

[135] When they realized this, they reasoned to themselves: "This man won't lay his own hands on public money and won't let us do so either. He'll be on the look-out and prevent us from distributing public money among ourselves. Besides that, if he catches any of us committing an offense, he'll bring him before an Athenian court and ruin him. So he must be got out of our way, justly or unjustly." [136] That's what they needed to do, gentlemen of the jury. But you need to do the opposite. I should like you to have as many men like me as possible, and my opponents to be eradicated, or at least to face some men who won't permit their activities. These should be men who are of

---

panhellenic festivals, such as the Isthmian games (held at the Isthmus of Corinth) and the Olympic games.

[112] This is one of the earliest references to a man who became a prominent politician in the 390s.

[113] Probably a tax on imports. The right to collect it was sold by the state by auction each year to an individual or a group of individuals. What Andocides now goes on to describe is the formation of a "ring" among the bidders to keep the price down illegally.

[114] This location is unknown.

good character and treat the people fairly, and they'll be willing and able to serve you well. So I promise you I'll either stop what Agyrrhius and his friends are doing and make them honest men, or bring before you for punishment those of them who are committing offenses.

[137] They also accused me about my sea voyages and commerce.[115] They said the reason why the gods preserved me in danger was, apparently, to let Cephisius bring about my death when I reached Athens. As for me, Athenians, I don't believe the gods intend any such thing. If they thought I'd done them wrong, they wouldn't have let me go unpunished when they had me in the greatest danger. When are people in greater danger than crossing the sea in winter-time? Did the gods have me in that situation, with complete control over my life and property, and then let me live after all? [138] Couldn't they have seen to it that my body wasn't even given burial? And again, there was a war on. There were always triremes at sea, and pirates too; many people were taken prisoner, lost their possessions, and spent the rest of their lives as slaves. Then there's foreign territory; many people before now have been wrecked on it, and after suffering the most terrible physical injuries have been put to death. [139] And did the gods keep me safe from these great dangers and then choose Cephisius to be their champion, the biggest scoundrel in Athens, who says he's an Athenian citizen when he isn't,[116] whom none of you who sit here would trust with anything of your own, because you know what sort of a man he is? No, gentlemen; I think we must take the view that dangers like my present ones are caused by human beings, and the dangers of the sea by the gods. If I must speculate about the gods, I think they'd be very angry and indignant to see men whom they'd kept safe being killed by other people.

[140] And you should also bear in mind, gentlemen, that at present the whole of Greece regards you as very generous and sensible men, because you didn't devote yourselves to revenge for the past, but to the preservation of the city and the unity of the citizens. Many others before now have suffered misfortunes just as bad as ours, but making

---

[115] This argument of the prosecution is found in the surviving speech *Against Andocides* (Lys. 6.19).

[116] If it were not for the amnesty, Cephisius would be disfranchised (1.92–93).

a satisfactory settlement of mutual disagreements has naturally been thought to be the thing for generous and reasonable men to do. So, since you possess these qualities, as is agreed by friend and foe alike, don't change your policy; don't deliberately deprive the city of this reputation or make people think you cast your votes more by chance than by judgment.

[141] I ask you all to take the same view of me as of my ancestors, and give me a chance to imitate them. Remember that they were equal to the city's greatest heroes and benefactors. Of all their reasons for acting as they did, the most important were their patriotism and their wish that, if they or any of their descendants ever got into any danger or trouble, they would be protected and forgiven by you. [142] It would be natural for you to remember them, because the city as a whole also owed a great deal to your own ancestors. After the navy was destroyed,[117] gentlemen, many people wanted to inflict permanent damage on Athens. But the Spartans, even though they were then our enemies, decided to preserve the city because of the brave actions of those men who laid the foundations of freedom for the whole of Greece.[118] [143] So, since Athens as a whole was preserved because of the brave actions of your ancestors, I think the brave actions of my ancestors should lead to my salvation too. My ancestors made no small contribution to those very achievements for which Athens was preserved. Therefore it is just for you to give me too a share in the safety which the Greeks extended to you.

[144] Consider too what a good citizen you'll be keeping, if you acquit me: one who first, after being very rich (you know how rich I was), became very poor and destitute, not through any fault of my own but because of the misfortunes of Athens, and later made myself a new living by honest means, with my own wits and my own hands; and also one who understands what it is to be a citizen of this great city, and understands what it is to be an alien living in a foreign country, [145] who knows the meaning of proper behavior and good sense, and knows the meaning of suffering for one's errors. I've mixed with

---

[117] In 405, at the end of the Peloponnesian War.

[118] In the Persian Wars, especially at the battle of Marathon in 490.

many people and had dealings with still more, and as a result I have ties of friendship with many kings, cities, and also private individuals abroad. If you acquit me, you'll be able to share them and make use of them whenever it suits you.

[146] It's like this, you see, gentlemen: if you put an end to my life today, you have no member of our family still left, but it perishes root and branch. Yet the house of Andocides and Leogoras is no disgrace to you by its existence. It was much more of a disgrace at the time when I was in exile and Cleophon the lyre-maker[119] lived in it. None of you when passing by our house has ever been reminded of any harm the members of my family have done you, either personally or officially. [147] They've very often been generals, and have been responsible for a large number of memorials of victories over your enemies by land and sea. They've very often held other offices and handled public money, and have never been found guilty of misconduct. No offense has ever been committed by us against you or by you against us. Our house is among the oldest of all, and always open to anyone in need. And none of my family has ever been brought to trial and asked you to show gratitude for these services. [148] So don't forget their achievements just because they themselves are dead. Remember their services, and imagine you can see them in person, asking you to save me. Who else can I bring forward to plead for me? My father? He is dead. My brothers? I have none. My children? They are not yet born. [149] You must be my father and brothers and children. It's to you that I come for protection, and appeal, and plead. You must make the request to yourselves, and save me.

You're ready to give Athenian citizenship to Thessalians and Andrians, because of the shortage of men. So don't at the same time put to death acknowledged citizens, who should be men of good character and are willing and able to be so; don't do that. And I also ask you to show your appreciation of what I do for you. If you do as I ask, you won't lose any services I can do for you; but if you do as my opponents ask, even if you change your minds later on, it won't be any good then.

---

[119] The most prominent Athenian politician in the closing years of the Peloponnesian War.

[150] So don't deprive yourselves of what you hope for from me, nor me of my hopes in you.

And now I'll ask these men, who have already given you proof of their outstanding patriotism, to come up here and advise you by giving their opinions about me. Come forward, Anytus[120] and Cephalus,[121] and also the members of my tribe appointed to support me, Thrasyllus and the others.

---

[120] One of the prosecutors of Socrates in 399. He appears as a character in Plato's *Meno*.

[121] See 1.115n.

2. ON HIS RETURN

〰〰〰〰〰〰〰〰〰〰〰〰〰〰〰〰〰〰〰〰〰〰〰〰〰〰〰〰〰〰〰〰〰〰〰〰〰〰〰

The speech *On His Return*, though placed second in the principal manuscript of Andocides, is earlier in date than *On the Mysteries*. After going into exile in 415 BC Andocides made his first attempt to return to Athens in 411. Thinking that the best way to persuade the Athenians to forgive him was to do them some service, he obtained some Macedonian timber for oar-spars and sold it at cost to the Athenian fleet then stationed at Samos. He went on from there to Athens, hoping to receive pardon for his activities in 415, but he found that he had arrived at the wrong moment. The oligarchy of Four Hundred, headed by Peisander, had just seized power, and was repudiated by the democratic sailors at Samos, so that Andocides' good turn to the fleet was taken as a hostile act towards the Four Hundred. So far from rewarding him, Peisander had him imprisoned.

Eventually, perhaps at the downfall of the Four Hundred, he was released, but he had to go into exile again. Some time after the restoration of democracy in 410 he made another attempt. He came to Athens and persuaded the Prytaneis to allow him to address the Assembly. This was the speech *On His Return*. The exact date of the speech is not known, but it must be between 410 and 405.

It is notable that in this speech he is more inclined to admit some guilt than in *On the Mysteries* a few years later: for example, he speaks of "my own youthfulness and folly" (7); he says "a very small part of the blame was mine" (8), and "I was in disgrace with the gods" (15). But these admissions are in vague terms, and he gives no precise account of what he has done. The main point of the speech is to claim that, through his good offices, a large number of grainships will shortly reach Athens from Cyprus, and that this should be regarded as compensation for his past errors. But it seems that this was not enough to win the Athenians' favor. He had to go into exile once again, and was not able to return to Athens permanently until 403.

2

[1] On any other subject, gentlemen, I shouldn't think it at all surprising if the speakers didn't all express the same opinion. But when it's a case of my doing a service to Athens—or if some less worthy person than myself wanted to do one—it seems to me quite extraordinary if one person is in favor and another not, and they're not unanimous. If the city belongs to all its citizens, surely services done to the city belong to them all too. [2] Well, you can see some men are already taking this very strange course, while others soon will. I simply can't understand why they flare up so strangely if you're to get the advantage of some service of mine. They must be either the stupidest men in the world or the city's worst enemies. If they think the prosperity of Athens would benefit their own private business, it's very stupid of them now to press for what is contrary to their own interests. [3] But if they consider that their own interests are not the same as the public interest, they must be enemies of Athens.

In fact when I made a report to the Council in secret session about actions which will be of the greatest possible advantage to the city if they're carried out, and gave the Councilors clear proof of them, though some of these men were present, none of them was able then to disprove anything I said, and neither was anyone else; but now they're trying to discredit me here. [4] This shows they aren't doing it of their own accord, or they'd have opposed me straightaway on that occasion. They're instigated by other men, such as do exist in Athens, who wouldn't for anything allow you to receive any benefit from me. Those men don't dare to come forward in public and make a statement in person on the subject, because they're afraid of being shown up as unpatriotic. They send other men in as their agents, men who are already so brazen that they don't care how much they insult people or get insulted. [5] All their case boils down to, you'll find, is sneering at my troubles in general—even though you, of course, are well aware of them already, so that they don't deserve any credit for any of it.

Personally, gentlemen, I agree with whoever it was who first said that all mankind is born for good and bad fortune. And I suppose that to err is a great misfortune, [6] and the most fortunate are those who err least, while the most sensible are those who realize their errors soonest. There's no distinction between some who err and others who don't; error and failure are common to everyone. So, Athenians, you'd be more considerate men if you judged me by human standards. My past life deserves sympathy rather than hostility. [7] I was so ill-starred—shall I say because of my own youthfulness and folly, or because of the influence of the people who persuaded me into such lunacy?—that I was compelled to choose between two terrible alternatives.[1] If I refused to reveal the men who did it, I had not only to dread what was to happen to me, but also to cause my innocent father's death along with my own, which he couldn't escape if I refused to do this. But if I revealed the facts, I should be released myself and escape death, and also I shouldn't become my father's murderer; and what wouldn't a man venture to do to avoid that?

[8] So in the circumstances I chose the course which for me would bring a long period of unhappiness, but for you a very quick end to your immediate difficulty. Remember what danger and despair you were in. You were so terrified of one another that you'd even stopped going out into the Agora, each of you thinking he was going to be arrested. For getting things into that condition, it was found that only a very small part of the blame was mine; for getting them out of it, I alone was the one man responsible. [9] Yet I can't help being the most unfortunate of men. When Athens was being drawn into these troubles, no one was heading for a worse fate than I was, and when it was beginning to be safe again I was unhappier than anyone. The city was in such a bad way, and there was no cure for it except by my disgrace; my ruin meant your salvation. So it's reasonable for you to thank me, not hate me, for that piece of bad luck.

[10] My troubles were perfectly clear to me at the time. I think there was no hardship or disgrace that I escaped, partly from my own idiocy and partly from force of circumstances. So I decided that the best thing was to take up activities and residence in a place where I

---

[1] Andocides avoids saying that the alternative which he chose was to betray his friends. The dilemma is expounded more fully in 1.51–60.

would very seldom be seen by you. But when some time later I began, naturally, to long for my old life as a citizen with you, which I exchanged for this one, I decided it was best for me either to put an end to my life or to do this city some service great enough to enable me at last, with your consent, to live among you as a citizen.

[11] Since then I've never failed to risk my person or my property when necessary. At once I imported some oar-spars to your forces at Samos, at the time when the Four Hundred had seized control of affairs in Athens,[2] since Archelaus[3] was a family friend of mine and gave me permission to cut down and export as many as I liked. I imported those spars, and though I could have had a price of 5 drachmas for them, I refused to take more than they cost me. I also imported grain and bronze. [12] The navy, equipped from those supplies, later defeated the Peloponnesians at sea,[4] and this city was saved by them alone at that time. So if their actions were of great benefit to you, I deserve not a little of the credit. If those men hadn't been brought the necessary supplies at that time, they'd have been facing danger not so much to save Athens as to avoid losing their own lives.

[13] This being so, I was quite surprised at the situation I found here. I sailed back expecting to be praised by people in Athens for my energy and patriotism. But when some of the Four Hundred heard I'd arrived, they looked for me at once, arrested me, and brought me before the Council. [14] Immediately Peisander stood beside me and said: "Gentlemen of the Council, I denounce this man before you for having transported grain and oar-spars to the enemy." Then he told them the whole story. By that time it was obvious that the servicemen held opposite views to the Four Hundred. [15] When I saw what an uproar was breaking out among the Councilors and realized I was done for, I at once leaped to the altar and took hold of the sacred objects.[5] This turned out to be a very good move; for though I was in disgrace with the gods, they seem to have had more pity on me than men, and when men wanted to kill me, it was the gods who saved my life.

---

[2] In 411, when the oligarchy was in power in Athens, the navy stationed at Samos continued to support democracy.

[3] King of Macedonia, which was rich in timber.

[4] At the battle of Cyzicus in 410.

[5] Andocides means that he sought sanctuary.

The imprisonment and terrible physical hardships that I endured afterwards would take too long for me to tell. [16] That was when I was most sorry for myself. On the one hand, when it was thought that the people of Athens were being harmed, harm was inflicted on me in return; on the other hand, when it was clear that I'd done the people good, I was being destroyed once again for that too. So I had no way or means left of keeping up my spirits. Whichever way I turned I could see I had a hard time in store. Nevertheless, when I got over this terrible experience, I still wanted above all else to do this city some service.

[17] You must realize, Athenians, how much actions like mine surpass ordinary services. When the citizens who administer your affairs disburse money for you, aren't they just giving you what belongs to you? Again, when men who are made generals accomplish some fine achievement for the city, don't they use your own physical hardship and danger, and expenditure of public funds as well, to do you whatever service it may be? And if they go wrong in the course of it, they don't pay for their error themselves; you pay for their errors. [18] Nevertheless they're awarded crowns by you, and they're proclaimed to be great men. And I won't say they don't deserve it. It's very meritorious for anyone to serve his city in any way he can. But still you must understand that much the most deserving man is the one who risks his own money and life in venturing to do a service to his fellow-citizens.

[19] Well, what I've done for you in the past, you'll practically all know. What I shall do in the future, and am already doing, five hundred of you[6] know in secret, and they're surely much less likely to make a mistake than if you were told now and had to reach a decision at once. They consider reports at leisure, and if they make a mistake they can be blamed and criticized by the other citizens. But there's no one else by whom you might be criticized; your affairs are rightly in your own hands, to conduct well or badly as you like.

[20] However, you shall hear what I'm able to tell you without giving away the secrets, because it's already done. You remember, I'm sure, that it was reported to you that no grain would arrive here from Cyprus. Well, I've been so successful that the men who planned and

---

[6] The members of the Council.

carried out this scheme against you have failed to accomplish their aim. [21] How this was achieved, it's not important for you to hear, but what I want you to know now is that you have fourteen grain ships which will be putting in to Piraeus at any moment, and the rest of the ships that sailed from Cyprus will arrive together soon afterwards. I'd give any money to be able to disclose to you safely what I reported to the Council in secret session, so that you'd know immediately what to expect. [22] As it is, you'll learn about it when it's completed, and receive the benefit of it at the same time. But now, Athenians, if you'd agree to do me a small favor in return, an act of justice that will give you no trouble, it would please me very much indeed. How just it is, you'll understand. It's something which you yourselves deliberately promised and gave me, but which you later, under the influence of other men, took away; that's the thing which, if you're willing to give it to me, I ask as a favor, but if you're not willing, I claim it as a right. [23] I've often seen you giving citizenship and large grants of money to slaves and foreigners of every country, if they do you some clear service. It's sensible of you to make these gifts, for in that way you'll receive services from a very large number of people. Now this is all that I'm asking you for: restore the decree which you passed on the proposal of Menippus, that I should have immunity.[7] He'll read it to you; the inscribed record still exists to this day in the Council-house.

[DECREE]

[24] That decree which you've just heard, Athenians, you passed for me, and then later took away from me as a favor to someone else.[8] So please do as I ask, and give up now any prejudice which any of you may feel against me. A person's body is not to blame for his errors of judgment; and in my case my body, which has been freed from blame, is still the same, while my judgment is changed now from what it was

---

[7] The decree passed in 415, granting Andocides immunity from prosecution in return for giving information about the mutilation of the Herms. Nothing else is known about Menippus.

[8] By the decree of Isotimides, which had the effect of nullifying the benefit of the decree of Menippus. Contrast 1.71, where Andocides denies that the decree of Isotimides applied to him.

before. So there's no good reason left now for you to be prejudiced against me. [25] At the time of my error you said you must treat my actions as the most reliable evidence, and concluded that I was a bad man; so now don't look for any other proof of my good intentions but the evidence you have of my present actions. [26] They're much more characteristic of me than my actions then, and more typical of my family. I'm not lying (the older men among you, at least, I can't take in by lying about it) when I say that my father's great-grandfather, Leogoras, led a revolt of the people against the tyrants.⁹ Though he might have made friends with the tyrants, married into their family, and joined with them in ruling the city, he preferred to be banished with the democrats and endure hardship in exile, rather than become a traitor to them. So my ancestors' actions too should make me a democrat, if I've now come back to my senses. Therefore, if you can see I'm a man who serves you well, you should accept what I'm doing more enthusiastically.

[27] Your giving me immunity and then taking it away, let me tell you, has never made me feel indignant. After all, you were persuaded by those men¹⁰ to do yourselves the greatest wrong, exchanging empire for slavery and turning democracy into dictatorship; so why should any of you be surprised that you were persuaded to do me wrong too? [28] But just as in your own affairs, as soon as you could, you invalidated the measures of the men who deceived you, so too, with regard to the inappropriate decision which you were persuaded to take about me, I should like you to make their decision ineffectual, and neither in this nor in anything else ever to vote on the same side as your own worst enemies.

---

⁹ If the text is correct, this Leogoras is a different ancestor from the one mentioned in 1.106; but some scholars think either that there is a scribal error in the text or that Andocides himself is confused.

¹⁰ The Four Hundred.

3. ON THE PEACE WITH SPARTA

〰〰

In 404 BC Athens was finally defeated by Sparta in the Peloponnesian War. The Athenians were compelled to demolish their town walls, to relinquish their empire and all their navy except twelve ships, and to install the oligarchic government of the Thirty. The oligarchy did not last long, and democracy was restored in 403; but the other restrictions continued, and rankled. The Spartans now dominated Greece, but their arrogance alienated even their former supporters. The consequence was that Athens, Boeotia, Corinth, and Argos formed a coalition against Sparta, and a new war, called the Corinthian War, began in 395.

The Spartans won some battles, but without decisive effect. The Athenians meanwhile were rebuilding their walls and their navy, and began to reassert their control over some of the islands. By 392 the Spartans considered that they had nothing to gain by prolonging the war. They hoped that a general peace could be arranged with the approval of the King of Persia. Xenophon (*Hellenica* 4.8.12–15) describes some negotiations which took place at Sardis, and subsequently a conference was held at Sparta to consider proposed peace terms. Athens was represented at it by four delegates: Epicrates, Andocides, Cratinus, and Eubulides. The appointment of Andocides shows that he must have reestablished himself in Athens very effectively since his acquittal eight years before, and indeed the smoother style of *On the Peace* suggests that he may have had more practice in public speaking since composing *On the Mysteries*.

The Athenian delegates had been given authority to conclude a treaty in Sparta, but instead of doing so they brought the proposed terms back to Athens for approval, perhaps because they suspected that they would be criticized for accepting them. The speech we have is the one that Andocides made to the Assembly in Athens recommending acceptance, probably in the winter or spring of 391. It is not known whether the other three delegates also spoke or Andocides was the spokesman for them all.

The terms offered to Athens included the lifting of three restrictions which Sparta had imposed in 404: the Athenians would now be permitted to rebuild their walls, to enlarge their navy beyond the limit of twelve ships, and to resume control of three islands in the north of the Aegean sea, Lemnos, Imbros, and Scyros. Greek cities in Asia were to remain under Persian control; other Greek cities were to be independent. Andocides in his speech argues that these terms give the Athenians all they need, so that continuation of the war would be pointless. We do not have the speeches of his opponents, but we can see from his arguments what their main points must have been. They evidently hoped for the reestablishment of the Athenian Empire in the Aegean, and they considered that restriction of Athenian control to only three islands would be insufficient to safeguard Athenian food supplies. The rebuilding of the walls and navy was already under way in any case, without a peace treaty. Above all, they evidently were afraid that alliance with Sparta would endanger the democratic constitution of Athens. It was the Spartans who had imposed the oppressive regime of the Thirty in 404, and no doubt Andocides' own aristocratic origin and his involvement in the scandals in 415 still aroused suspicion of his motives in advocating friendship with Sparta.

We know the upshot from Demosthenes (19.277–279) and from a fragment of the historian Philochorus (*F.Gr.Hist.* 328 F149a). Not only did the Athenians reject the proposed peace terms, but the delegates were accused of disobeying their instructions, making false reports, and accepting bribes; they fled to avoid trial and were condemned to death in their absence. Thus Andocides became an exile once again, and nothing is known of his life afterwards. The Corinthian War continued until 386, when the King's Peace was concluded on terms not very different from those proposed in 391.

For discussion of the speech, see especially Anna Missiou, *The Subversive Oratory of Andokides* (Cambridge, 1992).

3

[1] A just peace is better than a war, Athenians, as I think you all agree. But what you don't all realize is that the politicians, though they are nominally in favor of peace, are opposing the steps by which peace might be brought about. They say there's a very serious risk to democracy, if peace is made, that the present constitution may be subverted. [2] Now, if the people of Athens had never made peace with Sparta before, it would be natural to be apprehensive because of our inexperience of it and our distrust of Sparta. But since you've often made peace before now in times of democratic government, surely it's reasonable for you to consider first what happened on those previous occasions. The right thing to do, Athenians, is to use the past as evidence for the future.

[3] At the time when we were at war in Euboea, and we held Megara and Pegae and Trozen, we wanted peace.[1] We recalled Miltiades son of Cimon, who had been ostracized and was then in the Chersonese, for the very purpose of sending him to Sparta—he being Sparta's representative in Athens—to open negotiations for a truce. [4] On that occasion we made peace with Sparta for fifty[2] years, and both sides kept this truce for thirteen years. Let's consider this one case first. During that peace, was the Athenian democracy ever subverted? No one can show it was. But let me tell you what advantages we gained by that peace. [5] First, we fortified Piraeus during that period. Next, we built the northern Long Wall.[3] In place of the triremes we had then, which were old and unseaworthy—the ones in which we beat the King of Persia and his barbarians and made Greece free—in place of those ships we built 100 new triremes. That was when we first established a force of 300 horsemen and purchased 300 Scythian archers. Those were the advantages for the city and the power for the Athenian democracy which were produced by the peace with Sparta.

---

[1] Andocides now proceeds to give examples from the period 478–404. Although the general tenor of his argument is reasonable, the historical details are extremely inaccurate.

[2] The manuscripts here say "five"; but Aeschines 2.172, apparently copying from Andocides, says "fifty," and so editors alter the text of Andocides to match.

[3] See 1.45n.

[6] After that, war broke out because of Aegina. When we'd suffered and inflicted a good deal of damage, we wanted peace again, and
ten men, chosen from all the citizens of Athens, were appointed as
delegates to Sparta with full powers to negotiate about peace. Among
them was Andocides, my grandfather. They made peace with Sparta
for us for thirty years. In all that time, Athenians, was the democracy
ever subverted? Or were any people caught plotting the subversion of
the democracy? There's no one who can show that. [7] Quite the contrary: that peace raised the Athenian people to such heights, and made
us so strong, that first, in those years when we'd got peace, we stored
up 1,000 talents on the Acropolis and laid it down by law that they
were to be kept as a reserve for the people; and also we built 100 more
triremes and decreed that they were to be kept as a reserve; and we
built ship-sheds, and we established a force of 1,200 horsemen and the
same number of archers; and the southern Long Wall was built. Those
were the advantages for the city and the power for the Athenian democracy which were produced by the peace with Sparta.

[8] We went to war again because of Megara and allowed the countryside to be devastated. After many privations we again made peace,
which Nicias son of Niceratus arranged for us. I expect you all know
that that peace enabled us to store up 7,000 talents in coins on the
Acropolis. [9] We acquired over 400[4] ships; over 1,200 talents of tribute were coming in every year; we held the Chersonese, Naxos, and
more than two-thirds of Euboea; and it would take too long to list the
other colonies individually. With all those advantages we again went
to war with Sparta, persuaded by the Argives that time too.

[10] So first, Athenians, remember what I told you at the beginning
of my speech. It was simply this: that the Athenian democracy was
never subverted because of peace. Well, that's been demonstrated, and
no one can prove that what I say isn't true. But I've heard some people
say it was due to the last peace with Sparta that the Thirty were put
in power, and many Athenians died by drinking hemlock, and others
fled into exile. [11] Those who say that are wrong. There's a big difference between a peace and a truce. A peace is made on equal terms by

---

[4] Most editors emend this to "300," to match the figure in Aeschines 2.175.
Reasons for retaining "400" are given in *Classical Review* 15 (1965): 260.

people who have reached agreement about their disputes. A truce is made when the winners in the war dictate to the losers, as when the Spartans won the war against us and commanded us to demolish our walls, surrender our ships, and let our exiles return. [12] So on that occasion a truce was forced on us by their command, but now you're discussing a peace. Compare the actual written words—the ones inscribed for us on the stone[5] and the terms on which we can make peace now. In the inscription there, we have to demolish our walls: in these terms, we can rebuild them. There, we're to keep twelve ships: now, as many ships as we like. Then, Lemnos, Imbros, and Scyros are to be kept by those who held them at the time: now, they're to be ours. Now, we're not required to let any of the exiles return: then, we were required to, with the result that the democracy was subverted. What resemblance is there between these terms and the others? On this question, Athenians, I should go so far as to make this distinction: peace means safety and power for the democracy, while war means democracy's subversion. So much for that point.

[13] Some people say that at present it's necessary for us to go on with the war. First, then, Athenians, let's consider what the purpose of the war is to be. I suppose everyone would agree that there are two reasons for war: either because you're the victims of injustice, or because you're supporting the victims. Well, we were ourselves victims of injustice, and we were supporting the Boeotians who were victims. So if we've secured from Sparta an end to the injustice against us, and if the Boeotians are resolved to make peace, letting Orchomenus[6] be independent, what are we to make war for? [14] To make Athens free? But she already is. To get ourselves walls? But the peace gives us those too. To be able to construct triremes, and repair and keep the ones we have? We have that also, because the treaty makes cities autonomous. To take over the islands, Lemnos, Scyros, and Imbros? It's explicitly stated that they're to belong to Athens. [15] Well, to recover the Chersonese, our colonies, our estates abroad, and our debts? But neither the King of Persia nor our allies agree that we should do that, and we

---

[5] The terms inscribed on stone are those of the truce made in 404.

[6] A small city in northern Boeotia. The Boeotians had been claiming authority over it, but the Spartans championed its independence.

should need their help in a war to achieve it. "But we must go on fighting until we've beaten the Spartans and their allies." But I don't think we're equipped for that; and if we do accomplish it, what do you think the barbarians will do to us in our turn when we've done it? [16] So if that were the object of the war, and we had enough money and strong forces, even then we ought not to go on with the war. But if we have neither purpose nor opponents nor resources for war, shouldn't we make peace in whatever way we can?

[17] Consider this point too, Athenians. You're now bringing about peace and freedom for all Greeks alike, and you're giving them all a chance to share in every advantage. Think of the manner in which the greatest cities are ending the war. First the Spartans: when they began the war against us and our allies they commanded both the land and the sea, but now the peace is leaving them neither. [18] And they're not letting them go under compulsion from us, but to give freedom to the whole of Greece. They've won three battles now: first at Corinth against the full forces of all the allies, leaving us no excuse, but just because they were the best soldiers;[7] secondly in Boeotia, when Agesilaus was in command of them, they won a victory in the same way again;[8] and thirdly when they captured Lechaeum, against all the Argive and Corinthian forces and part of ours and the Boeotians'.[9] [19] After such a display of strength, they're ready to make peace keeping only their own territory, although they won the battles, and leaving the cities independent and the sea open to the losers. But what sort of a peace would they have got from us, if they'd lost even a single battle? [20] Again, how are the Boeotians making peace? They went to war because of Orchomenus; they said they wouldn't allow it to be independent. But now, after so many of their men have been killed and part of their land has been devastated, after they've paid out a great deal of private and public money, which is now a dead loss, after four years of war, they're still letting Orchomenus have its independence and are making peace, and they've gone through all that for nothing—because they could have let Orchomenus have its indepen-

---

[7] Sometimes called the battle of Nemea, in 394.
[8] The battle of Coronea, also in 394.
[9] In 393. Lechaeum was the western port of Corinth, linked to it by long walls.

dence at the start, and have stayed at peace. So that's the way in which they're ending the war.

[21] And what about ourselves, Athenians? How are we able to make peace? What's Sparta's attitude to us? Please excuse me if I hurt any of your feelings now; I'm only going to state the facts. First, when we lost our navy in the Hellespont and were confined inside our walls,[10] what proposal was made about us by those who are now our allies but at that time were allies of Sparta? Wasn't it to enslave our city and desolate our country? And who was it that prevented that happening? Wasn't it the Spartans, who persuaded their allies to change their minds and didn't even begin to discuss such action themselves? [22] After that we swore oaths to them and got them to agree to a stone inscription of the terms, which was the least infliction we could expect in the circumstances, and we observed a truce on specified conditions. Afterwards we formed an alliance, separating Boeotia and Corinth from them and resuming our friendly relations with Argos, and we involved them in the battle at Corinth. And who made the King of Persia hostile to them, and enabled Conon to fight the naval battle which caused them to lose command of the sea?[11] [23] Yet though we've treated them like that, they're still agreeing to the same terms as our allies and letting us have our walls, ships, and islands. What sort of peace, then, is the best that delegates can negotiate? Surely getting the same terms from the enemy as are offered by our friends, and achieving for our city the objectives for which we began the war? The rest of them are giving up part of what they have, in order to make peace, but we're getting just the things we want most.

[24] What is there still left to discuss? Corinth and the request the Argives are making to us. First, as far as Corinth is concerned, I should like someone to explain to me, if Boeotia isn't taking part in the war but is making peace with Sparta, what use is Corinth to us? [25] Remember, Athenians, the day when we made the alliance with Boeotia, and what we had in mind when we did that. Surely it was that the power of Boeotia combined with our own was enough to stand against the whole world. But now we're discussing how we can go on with the war against Sparta without Boeotia, since Boeotia is making peace.

---

[10] At the end of the Peloponnesian War, in 405 and 404.

[11] The battle of Cnidus in 394.

[26] "Yes, we can," say some people, "if we look after Corinth and have the Argives as allies." And if the Spartans attack Argos, shall we go to help Argos, or not? We shall certainly have to do one thing or the other. If we don't help, we have no argument left to show that we're not in the wrong and that the Argives aren't justified in doing whatever they like. But if we do help Argos, won't we find ourselves fighting against Sparta? To gain what? If we're defeated, to lose our own country as well as Corinth's; if we win, to give Corinth's to the Argives. Isn't that what we'll be fighting for?

[27] Let's look at what the Argives say. They tell us to go on with the war in alliance with themselves and the Corinthians, but they themselves have made a separate peace and don't allow the war to be fought in their territory. Though all our allies are joining us in making the peace, they say we shouldn't trust the Spartans; yet they say the Spartans have never broken the treaty which they made with them on their own. They call their peace traditional, but they don't let peace become traditional for the rest of Greece. They think that prolonging the war will enable them to annex Corinth, and when they dominate the city by which they've always been dominated, they hope their victorious allies will fall into line.

[28] Such are the prospects we face. We must choose one of two alternatives: either to join Argos and go on with the war against Sparta, or to join Boeotia in making peace. What I'm most afraid of, Athenians, is the mistake we keep on making: we always let our stronger friends go and give preference to the weaker ones, and we make war for other people when we could stay at peace for ourselves.

[29] First there was the King of Persia. (To reach a proper decision you have to remember what's happened in the past.) We made a truce with him and a treaty of everlasting friendship, which was negotiated for us by Epilycus son of Teisander, my mother's brother.[12] After that Amorges, the King's runaway slave, persuaded us to throw away the King's powerful support as if it were useless, and we gave preference to the friendship of Amorges in the belief that it was more important.[13] The King retaliated by becoming an ally of the Spartans and supplying

---

[12] Epilycus' negotiations with King Darius II took place in 424 or 423.

[13] Amorges was the leader of a rebellion in Caria against the King of Persia in 412.

them with 5,000 talents for the war, until he broke our power. That's one such decision that we made.

[30] Then there was the time when the Syracusans came with their request to us.[14] They wanted friendship instead of hostility, and peace instead of war; and they pointed out how much more valuable an alliance with them would be, if we were willing to make it, than one with Egesta and Catana. And that time too we chose war instead of peace, Egesta instead of Syracuse, and an expedition to Sicily instead of staying at home and having the Syracusans as allies. The result was that many of the bravest Athenians and allies were killed, a lot of ships, money, and resources were lost, and the survivors had a humiliating escape.

[31] Later the Argives, the same people who've come now to urge us to go on with the war, persuaded us to make a naval attack on Spartan territory,[15] though we were at peace with Sparta, and to display our spirit—the start of a series of disasters. At the end of the war which resulted we were compelled to demolish our walls, surrender our navy, and let our exiles return. And when that happened to us, what help did we get from the Argives who persuaded us to make war? What risk did they run for the Athenians? [32] So now the one thing left for us to do is to choose war this time too instead of peace, alliance with Argos instead of Boeotia, and the Corinthians who at present occupy Corinth instead of the Spartans! Please, Athenians, don't let anyone persuade us to do that. The examples of mistakes in the past are enough to prevent sensible men from making mistakes again.

[33] There are some of you who have this excessive desire for peace to be made as quickly as possible. They say even the forty days which you're allowed for discussion are a waste of time, and it was wrong of us to make this arrangement, because the reason why we were given full powers when we were sent to Sparta was to avoid reference back to you. Our caution in referring back they call cowardice. They say no one ever saved the Athenian people by openly convincing them; good service must be done by secrecy or deception. [34] I don't approve of

---

[14]Andocides is evidently referring to the events which led to the Athenian expedition to Sicily in 415, but the Syracusans' approach described here is otherwise unknown.

[15]This occurred in 414.

that argument. My opinion, Athenians, is that in wartime a patriotic and competent general does need to exercise secrecy and deception when he leads the ordinary people into danger; but when men are negotiating about peace for the whole of Greece, there shouldn't be any secrecy or deception about the conditions for which oaths will be sworn and inscribed stones set up. We deserve approval much more than criticism if, after being sent with full powers, we give you another opportunity to consider them. It's right to be as cautious as one can in reaching a decision; then, whatever we agree to on oath, we should keep to it.

[35] We delegates have to bear in mind not only our written instructions but also your own character, Athenians. You tend to be suspicious and disgruntled with whatever is available to you, and keep talking about what isn't available as if it were. If you have to fight a war, you want peace, and if someone arranges peace for you, you add up all the advantages you got from war. [36] So now some people are saying they don't know what sort of a reconciliation it is if the city gets walls and ships; they're not recovering their own private property from abroad, and they can't eat walls. So I must reply to this objection too.

[37] There was once a time, Athenians, when we had no walls or ships, but it was when we acquired them that our successes began. So if you want success again now, those are what you must have. With this foundation our fathers built up greater power for Athens than any other city has ever had. They dealt with Greece partly by persuasion, partly by secrecy, partly by bribery, and partly by force. [38] By persuasion it was arranged that Hellenotamiae[16] should be appointed at Athens to control the joint funds, that the fleet should muster here, and that we should supply triremes for those cities which had none; by secrecy the walls were built without the Peloponnesians' knowledge;[17] by bribery of the Spartans no penalty was paid for that; and by force against our opponents we established our Greek empire. Those are the successes we had in eighty-five years.[18] [39] But then we were de-

---

[16] Treasurers for the Delian League, which later became the Athenian Empire. Cf. Ant. 5.69n.

[17] The walls of Athens were rebuilt at the instigation of Themistocles after their destruction in the Persian Wars.

[18] From 490 to 405.

feated in the war, and among our other losses the Spartans demolished our walls and took over our ships, taking them as securities to ensure that we didn't have that foundation for rebuilding Athenian power. And now we've persuaded Spartan delegates with full powers to be here today, offering to give us back those securities, and agreeing that we should have our walls and ships and that the islands should belong to us.

[40] Now, though we're getting the same foundation for successes as our ancestors got, some people say this peace is unacceptable. They should come up and speak themselves, then; we've given them the chance, by getting an extra forty days for discussion. They should explain to you, on the one hand, if any part of the draft is unsatisfactory; it can be removed. And on the other hand, if anyone wants to add anything, he should convince you and put it in. If you accept the whole draft, you can be at peace. [41] If you don't like any of it, war is waiting for you. It's entirely up to you, Athenians; choose whichever you like. The Argives and Corinthians are here to tell you war is preferable, and the Spartans have come to urge you to make peace. The final decision rests with you, and not with Sparta—thanks to us. We delegates have made you all delegates. Each one of you who is going to raise his hand[19] is a delegate and will make peace or war, whichever he decides. So remember my words, men of Athens, and vote for a decision which will never cause you any regrets.

---

[19] To vote for or against the proposal.

4. AGAINST ALCIBIADES

〰〰

The speech *Against Alcibiades* purports to have been delivered on the occasion of an ostracism. In the fifth century BC ostracism was a method of banishing a citizen for ten years. Each year the question whether an ostracism should be held was put to the Assembly. If the people voted in favor of it, it was held in the Agora on a later day. Each citizen wishing to vote wrote on a fragment of pottery (*ostrakon*) the name of the man whom he wished to be banished. Provided that at least 6,000 citizens voted (or perhaps if at least 6,000 voted against the same man), the man with the largest number of votes was ostracized and had to go into exile for ten years.

The last time an ostracism was held was in 417, 416, or 415. It was expected that either Alcibiades or Nicias would be ostracized, but beforehand their supporters collaborated in urging people to vote against the less important politician Hyperbolus. The device was successful: Hyperbolus was ostracized, and Alcibiades and Nicias both avoided banishment. As a result, the system of ostracism fell into disrepute and was never used again.

This last ostracism appears to be the setting for the speech, in which Andocides (if he is the speaker) says that either Alcibiades or Nicias or himself will have to go into exile. But there are difficulties about assigning the speech to this date and this author. The following are some of the most serious.

1. The author of the speech does not have a correct understanding of how ostracism worked. He thinks that there were a number of candidates, one or other of whom must be exiled (2), whereas in fact there were no nominated candidates; each voter could vote against

anyone he wished, and if fewer than 6,000 votes were cast, no one would be ostracized at all. He envisages a meeting of the Assembly at which each candidate makes a speech (7), but in fact no meeting was held for this purpose. No one who lived in Athens in the period when ostracisms were held can have been so ignorant of the system.

2. In other ways too the author has an imperfect knowledge of Athenian politics in this period. He thinks that all Athenian citizens swore an oath (3), and that liturgies might be paid for out of public funds (42). He is almost certainly wrong in saying that Alcibiades was responsible for a doubling of the allies' tribute (11), that Hipponicus was killed at the battle of Delium (13), and that Alcibiades held a position of authority over the Athenian Empire (31).

3. The story that Alcibiades had a child by a Melian woman (22) implies that it is now at least nine months later than the fall of Melos, which occurred in the winter of 416/5; yet Alcibiades and Nicias both left Athens for the Sicilian expedition in the summer of 415. This leaves no possible date for the ostracism.

4. The speaker boasts that he has served as a delegate to six different places (41) and has performed various liturgies (42). But at the date of the last ostracism Andocides was only about twenty-five years old and cannot have done so much.

5. The style of the speech is perceptibly different from the style of Andocides' other speeches. In particular it makes more use of formal balance and antithesis.

Modern scholars have made various attempts to get over these difficulties. Hardly anyone now maintains that Andocides actually delivered the speech at the time of the last ostracism. Some have argued that it was delivered on that occasion by a different person; Plutarch, five centuries later, seems to have seen a copy of this speech in which it was attributed to the minor politician Phaeax (*Alcibiades* 13). Some have thought that it was written by Andocides for readers at a later date. But the evidence against it is cumulatively overwhelming. The best conclusion is that Andocides is not the author, and that the piece was written in later times as a literary exercise by someone trying to imagine what a speech at an Athenian ostracism might have been like.

For more detailed discussion of this question, with references to different views, see the edition of Andocides by Michael Edwards cited in the Introduction to Andocides.

4

[1] This isn't the first time I've realized how dangerous it is to take part in politics. I always did think it difficult, even before intervening in any public affairs. But I regard it as the duty of a good citizen to be prepared to take risks on behalf of the people, and not to be inactive in public for fear of personal opponents. Cities aren't made greater by men who mind their personal business; it's men who mind the state's business that make them great and free. [2] So I wanted to join their ranks, but it's got me into a very dangerous situation. Although I have excellent support from you to protect me, I have a large number of formidable opponents who slander me. So the present contest is not to award a crown,[1] but to decide whether a man who has done the city no harm must go into exile for ten years; and the competitors for this prize are myself, Alcibiades, and Nicias, one of whom must suffer this fate.

[3] It's fair to criticize the man who made this law[2] for framing it contrary to the oath of the people[3] and the Council. In the oath you swear not to exile or imprison or execute anyone without a trial, but on this occasion the man ostracized has to be excluded from the city for this long period with no accusation made nor defense granted nor voting in secret. [4] Secondly, these arrangements give an advantage to those who have a group of confederates, because the verdict is not given by men selected by lot, as in the lawcourts,[4] but all Athenians participate. Besides, the law seems to me in one way not to go far enough, and in another to go too far: I consider this an excessive penalty for private offenses, but for public ones I think it a small and negligible punishment, when it's possible to impose a fine or imprisonment or death. [5] Also, if anyone is removed because he's a bad citizen, he won't stop being one even when he's left Athens. Wherever he lives,

---

[1] A crown of leaves was the normal prize in an athletic contest.
[2] The law about ostracism.
[3] The citizens in the Assembly did not in fact swear an oath.
[4] In fact jurors were volunteers, but allocation to a particular court was by lot.

he'll harm this city and plot against it just as much, in fact even more, and with more reason, than before being expelled. I suppose this is the day that brings most sorrow to your friends and joy to your enemies, when they realize that, if you banish the best man by mistake, for ten years Athens will derive no benefit from him. [6] Another clear indication that it's a bad law is that we're the only people in Greece who have it; no other city is prepared to copy us. Yet the test of the best enactments is that they are found to be most suitable both for democracy and for oligarchy, and have the largest number of supporters.

[7] On that subject, I don't know that I need to speak at greater length; it would be no use at all in the present circumstances. But I want to ask you to preside over our speeches fairly and impartially, and all to act as Archons for them.⁵ Permit neither abuse nor cajolery, but be kind to one who is willing to speak and to listen, and hard on one who is insolent and clamorous. You'll make a better decision about us when you've heard the facts in each case.

[8] It remains for me to say a few words about being antidemocratic and seditious. If I hadn't been put on trial, naturally you would listen to my accusers and I should have to defend myself on these charges. But since I've been tried and acquitted four times, I don't think it's right for this subject to be discussed any further. Before a trial it's not easy to know whether accusations are false or true; but when a man has been acquitted or convicted, that's the end of it and the question is settled. [9] So I think it's terrible that men who have been convicted by only one vote are put to death and their property is confiscated, and yet men who win are subjected to the same accusations over again, and that jurors have power to destroy and yet appear to be powerless and incompetent to save, especially since the laws forbid a second trial of the same person on the same charge and you have sworn to apply the laws.

[10] Therefore I don't want to speak about myself, but to remind you about Alcibiades' life. Yet I really don't know where to begin: his misdeeds are so numerous, and all of them come to mind at once. Adultery, stealing other men's wives, and the rest of his violence and lawlessness—if I had to speak about them individually, the time available wouldn't be sufficient, and at the same time I should annoy many

---

⁵ Among other functions, Archons were chairmen in lawcourts.

citizens by making their misfortunes public. But I'll tell you about his activities concerning the city and his relatives and the other citizens and foreigners who have crossed his path. [11] First, when he'd persuaded you to reassess the cities' tribute, which had been assessed by Aristeides[6] as fairly as could be, and was appointed with nine other men to do that, he practically doubled it for each of the allies, and by showing himself to be formidable and powerful he contrived to get personal profit from the public funds. Just think: when our own safety is ensured entirely through our allies, and they're admittedly worse off now than they used to be, how could anyone contrive greater harm than by doubling the tribute for each of them? [12] So if you consider that Aristeides was a good and just citizen, you ought to think Alcibiades a very bad one, because his decisions about the cities were the opposite of Aristeides'. That's the reason why many men have left their own countries and become exiles, and have gone away to settle at Thurii.[7] The allies' hostility will become clear as soon as there's a war at sea between ourselves and Sparta. But I think a man is a bad leader if he concerns himself with the present and takes no thought for the future, and if he recommends the most popular policies in preference to the best ones.

[13] I'm surprised at people who are convinced that Alcibiades wants democracy, which seems to be the most egalitarian kind of constitution. They don't even draw conclusions from his personal life, although they can see how selfish and arrogant he is. He married the sister of Callias[8] with a dowry of ten talents, and after Hipponicus died as a general at Delium,[9] he made him pay ten more, saying that

---

[6] Aristeides "the Just" worked out originally the amounts of tribute to be paid annually to Athens by the cities in the Delian League, which subsequently became the Athenian Empire. The assessments were later increased, but there is no other evidence that Alcibiades was involved in increasing them.

[7] Thurii in south Italy was a new city founded at the instigation of Pericles in 443.

[8] Callias son of Hipponicus was the wealthy aristocrat who appears also in 1.112–132. His sister, the wife of Alcibiades, was named Hipparete.

[9] The battle of Delium was in 424. Athens was defeated by Boeotia, and the general Hippocrates was killed. There is no other evidence that Hipponicus was a general in that battle or died in it, and the writer has probably confused the two names.

Hipponicus had agreed to add that amount when Alcibiades had a child by his daughter. [14] But after receiving a larger dowry than any Greek ever had, he treated her in such an insulting manner, bringing mistresses, both slave and free, into the same house with her, that his wife, who was a very respectable lady, was compelled to leave him, going to the Archon as the law requires.[10] That was where he really did show his power: he called in his friends and carried his wife off from the Agora by force, making clear to everyone his contempt for the Archons, the laws, and the other citizens. [15] Even that wasn't enough for him, but he also plotted the murder of Callias in order to get possession of Hipponicus' estate. Callias made the accusation in the presence of all of you in the Assembly, and bequeathed his money to the people of Athens if he should die childless, because he was afraid of being killed for his property. However, Callias is neither friendless nor vulnerable; he can call on plenty of support because of his wealth. But when a man insults his own wife and plots the death of his brother-in-law, how must he be expected to behave towards other citizens who come into contact with him? Everyone considers his own family more important than anyone else's.

[16] But the worst thing of all is when a man like that makes out in his speeches that he favors democracy and calls other men oligarchical and antidemocratic. A man who ought to have been put to death for his behavior is selected by you to accuse people who have been slandered,[11] and he says he's a guardian of the constitution, although he thinks he should be neither equal nor only a little superior to any other Athenian. He has shown such utter contempt that he has continually flattered you in a body but insulted you individually. [17] He had the impudence to persuade Agatharchus the painter[12] to go to his house with him and force him to paint. Agatharchus pleaded, quite truly, that he couldn't do it now because he was contracted to other

---

[10] A woman wanting a divorce had to apply to the Archon.

[11] Apparently Alcibiades has accused the speaker or his friends of being antidemocratic, but the circumstances, if indeed they are historical at all, are unknown.

[12] A distinguished painter from Samos, who had worked on the buildings on the Acropolis. According to another version of this story (Dem. 21.147 and scholium) he had been caught in intercourse with Alcibiades' concubine, and this was regarded as justifying Alcibiades' treatment of him.

people, but Alcibiades threatened to imprison him if he didn't start painting straightaway. That's what he did, and Agatharchus didn't escape until after three months he evaded the guards and ran away—as if from the King of Persia! But Alcibiades is so shameless that he went to him and accused him of cheating him. He didn't apologize for using force, but threatened him for leaving the work unfinished. Democracy and freedom were no use, because he'd shut him up, just like those who are admittedly slaves. [18] It annoys me to think that for you it's not safe to arrest even criminals and take them to the prison, because of the rule that anyone who doesn't obtain one-fifth of the votes must pay 1,000 drachmas,[13] while Alcibiades hasn't been punished at all for imprisoning the man all that time and compelling him to paint; it seems to have made him even more haughty and terrifying. In legal treaties with other cities we agree that it should not be permitted to confine or imprison a free person, and we prescribe a heavy penalty for any transgressor; but no one makes Alcibiades compensate either an individual or the city for such conduct. [19] In my opinion the thing which protects everyone is obedience to the officials and to the laws. Anyone who ignores them has destroyed the city's greatest safeguard. It's bad enough to suffer harm from people who don't know what is right, but it's much harder to bear when someone does know what is important and transgresses it, because he's showing clearly, like Alcibiades, that he doesn't think that he should conform to the city's laws, but that you should conform to his inclinations.

[20] And remember Taureas,[14] who competed with Alcibiades as choregus of a chorus of boys. The law permits removing any competing chorister who is a foreigner, and no one may prevent a person who proceeds to do so; but in front of the audience of Athenians and other Greeks, and in the presence of all the officials in the city, Alcibiades hit him and drove him away. The spectators sided with Taureas and took a poor view of Alcibiades, and so they applauded the one chorus and refused to listen to the other. But Taureas gained nothing by it. [21] The judges awarded the prize to Alcibiades, some because they

---

[13] See 1.33n.

[14] This Taureas may be the relative of Andocides mentioned in 1.47. Apparently he tried to remove from Alcibiades' chorus a boy who was allegedly an alien and therefore not entitled to take part. Cf. Dem. 21.147.

were frightened and some to do him a favor. They thought him more important than their oath. I think it was natural for the judges to pander to Alcibiades, when they saw that Taureas, who had spent so much money, was abused, while Alcibiades, who committed such offenses, had the greatest power. You are to blame, because you don't exact penalties for insolence. You punish secretive crime, but you admire open bullying. [22] That's why the young spend their time not in the gymnasiums but in the lawcourts. While the older men serve in the army, the younger men make public speeches, following the example of this man. His offensive behavior goes beyond all bounds. After making a proposal for enslavement of the Melians,[15] he bought one of the female prisoners and had a son by her. That baby was born even more illicitly than Aegisthus:[16] his parents are each other's greatest enemies, and he has relatives of whom some inflicted and others endured the utmost suffering. [23] Let me make Alcibiades' audacity even plainer. He had a child by a woman whom he had made a slave instead of free, whose father and relatives he had killed, and whose city he had destroyed; thus he made his son a deadly enemy to himself and to Athens, so compelling are his motives for loathing them. But as for you, you think such deeds terrible when you see them in tragedies, but when you see them happening in Athens you don't care a scrap. Yet in the one case you don't really know whether they did happen in that way or have been invented by the poets; in the other case, when you know very well that these lawless deeds have been done, you tolerate them easily.

[24] And another thing: some people go so far as to say that there has never been a man like Alcibiades. But I think he'll do Athens the greatest harm, and in times to come he'll be blamed for trouble so great that no one will remember his earlier offenses. It wouldn't be at all surprising, when the first part of his life has been like this, if the later part were extraordinary too. Sensible men should beware of citizens who get above themselves, remembering that that's the sort of men who establish tyrannies.

---

[15] In 416, the Athenians took the island of Melos, put the men to death, and enslaved the women and children.

[16] See 1.129n.

[25] I think he won't make any reply to that; he'll talk about his victory at Olympia [17] and anything rather than a defense against the charges. But this very fact, as I shall show, makes it more appropriate for him to die than to live. I'll explain it to you. [26] Diomedes [18] took a pair of horses to Olympia; he was a man of moderate means, but he wanted to use them to bring a crown to his city and his house, and he reckoned that most horse races are decided by chance. Although he was a fellow-citizen, Alcibiades, who just happened to meet him and had influence with the Elean organizers of the games, [19] took away the pair and competed with it himself. Yet what do you think he'd have done if one of your allies had arrived with a pair of horses? [27] He'd have been very quick to allow him to compete against himself, I'm sure!—a man who used violence against an Athenian and had the nerve to compete with someone else's horses, showing the Greeks that he thought nothing of using violence against any of them, since he doesn't treat even fellow-citizens as equals: he robs some, hits others, shuts others up, gets money out of others, and shows that democracy is worth nothing, speaking like a demagogue and acting like a tyrant, because he's realized that you're concerned only about the word and not about the thing itself. [28] He's very different from the Spartans. They tolerate defeat even from their allies competing against them, but he doesn't tolerate it even from his fellow-citizens. He's said openly that he won't permit rivals in anything. That sort of behavior is bound to make the cities want to join our enemies, and hate us.

[29] To show he was insulting the whole city, not just Diomedes, after borrowing the processional vessels from the Architheori [20] for use at his victory celebration on the day before the sacrifice, he broke his word and refused to return them, because he wanted to use the gold

---

[17] At the Olympic games in 416 Alcibiades provided seven entries for the chariot race, three of which came first, second, and fourth.

[18] Isocrates 16, referring apparently to the same incident, gives the name of Teisias, a member of the Council under the regime of the Thirty. Possibly Teisias and Diomedes owned the horses jointly, or possibly the name of Diomedes (who is otherwise unknown) is simply a mistake.

[19] Elis was the nearest city to Olympia and undertook the organization of the festival.

[20] See 1.132n.

basins and censers the next day before the city did. So foreigners who didn't know they were ours, on seeing them used in Athens' procession, which was later than Alcibiades', thought we were using his vessels, while those who were told about his behavior by our citizens, or had observed it themselves, laughed at us when they saw that one man was more powerful than the whole city.

[30] Notice too how he arranged the rest of his visit to Olympia. The Ephesians pitched for him a Persian tent twice as big as the Athenian tent, the Chians supplied animals for sacrifice and fodder for his horses, and he requisitioned wine and the rest of his expenses from the Lesbians. All Greece has witnessed his lawlessness and corruption, and yet he's never been punished for it, because he's so successful. Men who have held office in one city undergo an examination of their conduct, [31] but Alcibiades, who holds office over all the allies and receives money,[21] is not subject to trial for any of this, but was rewarded for his behavior with maintenance in the Prytaneum.[22] Besides, he takes great credit for his victory, as if he hadn't brought dishonor to the city rather than a crown. If you look into it, you'll find that people who have done for a short time any one of the things that Alcibiades has done repeatedly have ruined their families, while he indulges in every extravagance and has become twice as rich as before. [32] You regard thrifty and parsimonious men as money-lovers, but you're wrong. It's the men who spend a great deal and have many wants who are the most avaricious. It will be an absolute disgrace if you put up with Alcibiades, who has spent your money on these activities, after ostracizing Callias son of Didymias without paying any attention to the fact that he brought honor to Athens by his own personal efforts in winning all the athletic contests for which crowns are awarded.[23] [33] Remember too the good sense of your ancestors, who ostracized Cimon for his lawless conduct because he cohabited with his own sis-

---

[21] The text is uncertain here, and it is not clear what office the writer may have had in mind.

[22] See 1.45n.

[23] Callias son of Didymias is known to have won the pancratium at Olympia in 472. The date of his ostracism is not known, but is likely to have been around 450 or later.

ter.[24] Yet not only was he himself an Olympic victor, but his father Miltiades was too. Nevertheless they didn't take his victories into account; they judged him not by the games but by his way of life.

[34] Then again, if our families ought to be taken into consideration, ostracism has nothing to do with me, and no one could show that this disaster ever happened to anyone in our family. But it has more to do with Alcibiades than anyone in Athens. His mother's father Megacles and his grandfather Alcibiades were both ostracized,[25] so that it won't be at all strange or surprising if it's thought right that he should be treated in the same way as his ancestors. Indeed not even he himself would attempt to deny that they, although more lawless than everyone else, were more sober and honest than he is, since no accusation could describe his misdeeds adequately.

[35] I think that the man who made the law also had this intention: he had in mind those citizens who are more powerful than the officials and the laws, and since it's impossible for an individual to punish such men, he arranged for them to be punished by the state on behalf of their victims. Now I've been put on public trial four times, and I haven't prevented anyone who wanted to prosecute me individually; but Alcibiades has never faced trial for the kind of thing he's done. [36] He's such a difficult man that they don't punish him for his past offenses for fear of what he'll do in the future; it's better for the victims to put up with him, and he won't be satisfied unless he can do whatever he likes in the future too. But surely, Athenians, I don't deserve ostracism when I've been judged not to deserve death, and when I've been acquitted in a trial I ought not to be exiled without trial, and after winning so many cases in court it wouldn't seem just for me to be banished for them now. [37] Still, perhaps it was a minor charge or weak prosecutors or commonplace opponents who placed me in jeopardy, not the most formidable men of speech and action, who brought about the death of two men facing the same charge as I was? Yet the men whom it's just to expel are not those whom you find innocent

---

[24] The real reason for Cimon's ostracism in 461 was probably his policy of cooperation with Sparta. The story of his incestuous relationship with his sister Elpinice may be mere slander.

[25] Megacles was ostracized in 486, Alcibiades the elder about 460.

after repeated examination, but those who refuse to submit to the city an account of their life. [38] It seems shocking to me: if someone wanted to speak in defense of the men who have been executed, arguing that they died unjustly, you wouldn't tolerate people trying to do that; and if the men who were acquitted are accused again on the same charge, surely it's right to take the same line about the living as about the dead.

[39] It's typical of Alcibiades to ignore the laws and oaths himself and encourage you to break them, to have no compunction in causing the expulsion and execution of other men but to plead and weep pitifully for himself. And that doesn't surprise me, because he's done plenty of things to make one weep; but I wonder who's really going to be convinced by his entreaties. The young? He's given them a bad name by bullying, putting the gymnasiums out of business, and acting beyond his years. Or the old? He hasn't adopted their life-style but has shown his contempt for their activities. [40] The important thing is not just that lawbreakers should be punished themselves, but that others should see it and so become more honest and better-behaved. Driving me out will terrify good people, but punishing Alcibiades will make bullies more law-abiding.

[41] I should like to remind you of what I myself have done. As a delegate to Thessaly, Macedonia, Molossia, Thesprotia, Italy, and Sicily, I got some people to end their disputes with you, others to establish friendly relations, and others to break off relations with your opponents. If every delegate did the same, you'd have few enemies and you'd possess many allies. [42] I don't think I should mention my liturgies,[26] except to say that I spend what is required not from public funds but from my own money. Yet I've gained victories in the contests of physique, torch-race, and tragedies—not by hitting the rival choregi, nor by being ashamed of being less powerful than the laws. Such citizens, I believe, are more fit to remain in Athens than to be exiled.

---

[26] See 1.132n.

INDEX